ON THE TRAIL!

A PRACTICAL GUIDE TO THE WORKING BLOODHOUND
AND OTHER SEARCH AND RESCUE DOGS

Jan Tweedie

Alpine
PUBLICATIONS
Loveand, CO 80537

ON THE TRAIL!

ISBN: 1-57779-005-7

Library of Congress Cataloging in Publication Data
Tweedie, Jan, 1957-
   On the trail! : a practical guide to the working bloodhound and other search and rescue dogs / Jan Tweedie. — 1st ed.
      p.   cm.
   Includes bibliographical references (p.   ) and index.
   ISBN 1-57779-005-7
      1. Bloodhounds—Training. 2. Search dogs—Training. 3. Rescue dogs—Training. I. Title.
SF429.B6T84 1997
636.753'6—dc21   97-46170
                                                                                    CIP

Many manufacturers secure trademark rights for their products. When Alpine Publications is aware of a trademark claim, we print the product name as trademarked or in initial capital letters.

Alpine Publications accepts no responsibility for veterinary medical information, suggested treatments or vaccinations mentioned herein. The reader is advised to check with their local, licensed veterinarian if at all possible before giving medical attention.

This book is available from the publisher at special quantity discounts for breeders, club promotions, premiums, or educational use. Write for details.

Printed in the United States of America

First Edition
10 9 8 7 6 5 4 3 2 1

Cover photograph: Ch. Det. Lawrence of Westvilla, "Digger," in action.
   by Jan Tweedie
Cover and interior design by:
   Dianne J. Nelson, Shadow Canyon Graphics

CONTENTS

FOREWORD

In researching my first novel I combed the stacks of public libraries, book stores, and "how to" magazine ads, searching for a definitive and comprehensive training manual on Bloodhounds. I was disappointed with what was available. If you want to train a Bloodhound for search and rescue, learn mantrailing, bone up on the latest techniques, or simply enjoy reading an interesting and exciting book detailing Bloodhound lore, you now have it in your hands. This is the book for you.

If not for the kindness of strangers—that wonderful, generous group of Bloodhound breeders, trainers, and owners—my books would not have clarity and the ring of truth. Jan Tweedie belongs to this elite band. She is an expert. I faintly hear her voice giving instruction and advice on every page. Many people think my fictional character is patterned on the life of Jan Tweedie, even though we've never met, and live on opposite coasts. So be it. My heroine Jo Beth and her Bloodhounds could not have a better mentor and role model.

Virginia Lanier
Agatha nominee for Best First Novel
Death in Bloodhound Red
The House on Bloodhound Lane

FOREWORD

W ith warm and funny anecdotes, author Jan Tweedie conveys the triumphs and tribulations of life with the working Bloodhound. Using her law enforcement, corrections, search and rescue and personal experience, Jan gives excellent advice on raising and training this breed, detailing the hard work and effort involved in producing a reliable search and rescue tool. Law enforcement personnel will find practical information for using the Bloodhound to locate a missing child.

Jan makes it very clear that there is no magic wand to train this wonderful "nose with a tail," but perhaps this book will prevent some of the whimsical purchases that result in too many dogs relegated to animals shelters and breed rescue groups.

For anyone that marvels at what nature and good breeding can create, this book is for them.

Mary E. Michener
Former Editor
American Bloodhound Club Bulletin

ACKNOWLEDGMENTS

To Digger, Swamp Angel, Jethro, Kady, Jonah, Ben, and now Kailey, the four-footed forever friends without whom this book would not have come about.

To Larry and Brian, who were involved when this whole thing got started, who worked with imagination, humor, creativity and versatility as we trained ourselves and the dogs.

To the Kittitas County Sheriff's Office which let me try theories and methods and which supported the use of Bloodhounds in all kinds of situations and crimes. To the Sheriff, who was known to regularly disappear with Digger to visit the Red Cross doughnut box. Thanks, Bob and Carl.

To the Corrections Officers who made sure the work got done as I raced into the hills with the dogs on another search, who supported and encouraged me and kept things together at the office.

To Lynn and Sid Harty, my partners and friends, for the hours of work and weekends of trailing practice, dog shows and searches. For the laughter, the commitment, the support and the encouragement. To Justin and Josh, who got to see all of these ideas happen and who spent hours walking dogs, giving hugs and playing with puppies.

To Crystal, who believed that Bloodhounds should work and show, who handled Digger in the ring and Angel on the trail, and who so beautifully captured my hounds in her art.

To Anne Legge for Kady and Kailey, my parts of the Legacy, for breeding and producing working show champions and for her support, loyalty and encouragement.

To Mary Michener for her encouragement, for her devotion to the breed, for her editing skills, and for the push to get this published.

To Sue Carpentier (and Decon and Blu), Julie and Patrick Cardinal (and Tory and Zipper), Rick and Rosemary, Ray and Kay, Suzi and my other good friends who took the time to read through draft after draft and who tried out the theories and ideas with energy and commitment.

To the Search and Rescue Coordinators and Law Enforcement officials who believe in the abilities of the hounds and who call time and time again for help.

To those who ran and walked, tried and tested, found victims and saved lives, solved crimes and worked and trained before me and for those who will carry on with hounds to come.

And finally to Mom and Dad, who supported and encouraged me and dealt with the slobbering hounds because they loved me.

PREFACE

As I write this, I am surrounded by my best friends. They curl up in front of the computer and across my feet, jostling each other for the best position. My feet become headrests for the noble brow, and the cadence of snoring comes quickly.

I remember the beginning like it was yesterday. In October of 1981, I was working as a Deputy Sheriff and among other responsibilities, I was assigned to Search and Rescue. On one particular weekend I responded to three searches. It was the beginning of hunting season, and all three of the victims ended up dead. One died from a vehicle wreck in which he was tossed down a mountainside, the second died of heart failure and the third died of exposure. In two of the three cases the missing person had to be located by searchers. The second hunter, who died in the field, required two days of searching to find. Before that weekend I never entertained the thought of working a dog in the field, but suddenly it became very apparent that something other than our "best guess," theories, and random searches would have to be used to find these people faster.

My friend Larry Allen and I decided to look into getting a search dog. We looked at both the German Shepherd dog and the Bloodhound as the top two breeds. We had both worked shepherds but neither of us had even seen a Bloodhound up close. We approached local community groups for funding, but in a small town, money is hard to come by. One night

Larry was reading a hunting magazine and came across an ad for Bloodhound puppies from Kansas. A few quick and frantic phone calls later, and we were waiting for a new little puppy to train. Waiting for Digger seemed like forever, but he finally arrived late in November of 1981.

We drove 125 miles to the airport and arrived about eight hours early. We spent the time fitfully, wandering from pet shop to pet shop, buying cute treats and toys for our new "child." The flight finally arrived and we stood anxiously next to the counter in the freight office hoping to catch a glimpse of the bouncing puppy. After a brief scare, when they said they didn't have any record of a dog on the flight, they carried out a big plastic kennel and set it down. There was nothing moving inside. No noise. Where was our "ball of fire" search puppy? Where was our search and rescue miracle worker? Was he sick, or had something unimaginable happened to him?

I leaned in close to the carrier and looked inside. Suddenly I heard snoring inside the crate. I opened the door and inside was a big lump of snoring, wrinkled Bloodhound. He was fast asleep and not at all pleased to be dragged from his warm nest by me. He whined and then promptly resumed snoring, resting on my shoulder. So much for a dramatic introduction to Ch. Det. Lawrence of Westvilla, a.k.a. Digger. My plans for a bundle of energy would have to wait until this nap and many more were through.

Digger weighed twenty-five pounds at seven weeks of age and grew steadily until he was two years old. He teethed on my recliner, brought me mouthfuls of puppy chow as gifts in the night, loved to be rocked and took to the trail like a duck to water. At two years old, he was twenty-six inches at the shoulder and weighed between 100 and 110 pounds. We regularly measured, weighed, and pampered and protected him throughout his adolescence only to find that we had encouraged his fear of loud noises, such as thunder, vacuum cleaners, weed eaters, gunfire and fireworks. We had created a very excellent search dog who loved to live inside the house.

Digger crossed the paths of many as he worked, searched, showed, discovered evidence, found criminals, solved cases, traveled and slumbered. He loved hearing the pager go off, whined as I loaded our working gear, "hummed" along with the music and was well known for his loud snoring and slumbering on even the noisiest helicopter. Digger loved searching, meeting children, and lying in the sun on the top of the hot tub.

Digger was a leader, an investigator, an ambassador and a companion. He was a clown and conspirator, a bed hog, a friend. Digger loved meeting people and introduced me to very special people throughout the world, crossing borders, cultures and languages. He found fault in no one. I don't think there was anyone he didn't like. Digger was the quiet, consistent presence in a sometimes crazy or tragic or dangerous chain of events, confident and consistent, mourning for those he couldn't help. On November 4, 1993 I held him as he died, old age finally claiming my friend of more than twelve years. I will forever miss him. There will always be a tremendous void where Digger lived.

I believe that a working dog should also be competitive in the conformation ring. Much to Digger's amusement, I forced him into the show ring where he quickly became a bored Champion. He always thought dog shows were quite interesting and he tended to clown around in the show ring. He would play all around the ring, jump up in the air, and once tried to jump a barrier and show with the Bouvier des Flandres across the way.

At our first show, it was time for him to stand for the judge. Digger decided it would be fun to roll over and play dead. Lucky for us, the judge thought he was very funny and he earned his first "Best of Breed." He finished his championship in less than a year. He was shown as a "special" from time to time until he was a "Veteran" at seven years old.

Digger's mom, Swamp Angel of Mercy, came to live with me about six months after Digger arrived. Angel required a lot of health care and nutritional devotion to get her in good shape but Angel loved to trail and soon mother and son became an unbeatable team. They trailed children, mental patients, fugitives, criminals, evidence, and lost adults, and they broke new ground in evidence acceptability in Washington State.

Gradually Angel developed spondylosis and was nearly blinded by cataracts as she approached her ninth birthday.

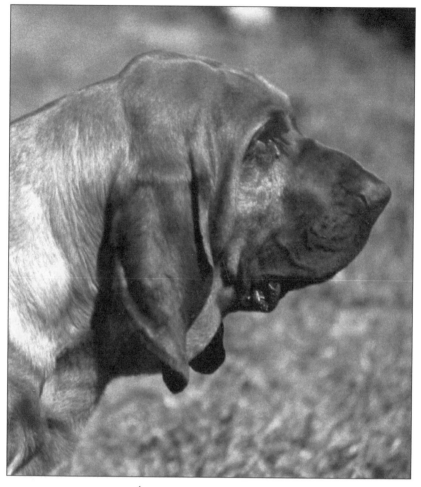

Digger. PHOTO BY JAN TWEEDIE

She survived bloat surgery, three non-surgical bloats, pyometra, cuts, wounds and a skull abscess. Despite all this she would not give up. She refused to retire and worked easier terrain up until a month before she died.

On July 5, 1989 I faced one of the hardest decisions in a dog handler's world. Nine-year-old Swamp Angel developed a tumor that spread so quickly that there was nothing anyone could do. I called the veterinarian and made an appointment, not wanting to believe it would be our last ride together. She seemed wiser and stronger that day and despite the cataracts, she seemed to see clearly.

I called her from the yard for the drive to the vet's office, and before she came to the door, she went up to each of the other dogs, nuzzling them quietly. Then, walking slower but with her head up, she came to me. My hands shook as I dropped the collar over her head and watched as she walked out the door to the car.

I lifted her into the car that had taken both of us to searches and crime scenes all over the region and she seemed to know that it was different this time. Instead of curling up to nap as the dogs always do on the way to a search, she stood quietly in the back, watching the world go by as we drove.

At the doctor's office, she wagged her tail and greeted everyone with her customary friendliness. I flashed back to the emergency visits we had made when she rousted an unfriendly porcupine, encountered an anti-social skunk, and had bloat surgery, a skull abscess, and the back injury. She had always bounced back, but that day she was quiet and seemed to be saying goodbye to her friends.

She stayed by my side, leaning against me as she always did. When it was clear there was nothing medically we could do to help her, I knew I had to let her go. I knelt down beside her and she leaned into me as she had a thousand other times in the past, but this time she nuzzled me as if to comfort me, as if she knew this was our last hug. As the needle slipped into her vein, she sighed and nestled in closer. I knew that a part of me was going with her, but that her spirit and undying devotion to the trail would always be a part of me.

Jonah was black and tan, with large ears that stuck straight up. Jonah represented another breed of search dog, the German Shepherd. Digger and Angel firmly believed he was an unfortunate-looking Bloodhound but accepted him as family; Jonah believed that Digger and Angel were pretty sorry-looking for Shepherds but, since they were family, I think he overlooked their droopy ears.

Jonah did well in his search training but chose to follow me while I worked the hounds. He excelled in obedience work. He was excellent at debriefing the hounds after a search and was a natural caretaker, endlessly fetching and throwing tennis balls for the puppies. He would carefully herd dozing puppies into the center of the yard and then curl protectively around them, watching over them as they slept. Always the attentive groomer, he carefully washed puppy faces after meals.

In early April 1994 Jonah developed acute spondylosis, causing him to drag one hind leg. He continued to chase his tennis ball and was a constant companion until late May of 1994 when his condition worsened. It felt like the longest walk ever as I took him to the vet to put him down.

Ch. Legacy-HKLDM F'Getmenot Kady, or "Kady" for short, was a black and tan Bloodhound who was full of the youthful mischief and bounce that Digger and Angel had traded for stamina. Kady eagerly accepted the harness and identified trailing as her mission in life; she was a hardworking, hardheaded, trailing addict. Kady trained me well. She had benefited from

Jonah. PHOTO BY JAN TWEEDIE

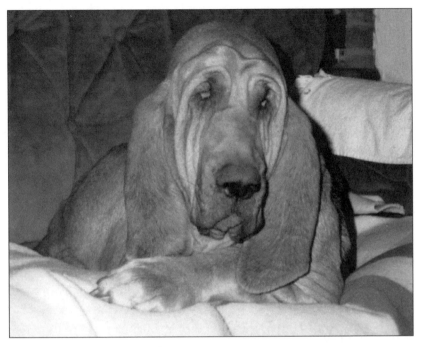

Kady. PHOTO BY JAN TWEEDIE

the trial-and-error training that Digger and Angel had endured.
She was impatient and relentless on the trail. Occasionally she
reminded me, unceremoniously, that *she* was the trailing dog
and that *she* would determine the trail, not me. More than
once I thought I knew better than she did. She would stop
working, sit down with her back to me and throw her head
back over her shoulder as if to say, "Well, if you're so smart,
you lead!" Needless to say, she was right. She celebrated the
end of a trail with wags, and loud choruses of "ROO!"

Kady collapsed and died as we walked out of the garage early
in March of 1994. The cause of death was a total collapse of her
body, including kidney failure and some other internal deficien-
cies. She had struggled with a thyroid problem since she was
two, and an autopsy revealed that she had no thyroid gland.

Kady's *Bulletin* memorial read, "Kady was the tyrant, the
school marm, the counter-cruising, egg-stealing thief, the self-

appointed queen, my shadow. Kady taught me to believe, introduced me to the legacy of Legacy, stole my heart, opened my eyes and trained me well. Kady was famous for her 'ROO!,' her dinner-pan dance, her pushy, nosy way of getting just about everything she wanted. Kady loved to boss everyone, no matter if they were two-legged or four-legged. She could slink up on the couch and shove people off so discreetly they didn't know what happened until they landed on the floor and heard the snoring on the couch. Kady was a show-off whether on the trail, during her show career, or walking around the block." I will always miss her.

Early in 1982 Larry and I were notified that there was a big, red male Bloodhound that had been abandoned in the Lewis County Dog Pound which would be donated to us if we would come and get him. We drove over through the icy pass and brought our third hound home, much to the amusement of the neighbors and the other dogs. Enter Jethro Bodine.

Jethro had been badly abused and carried a hip injury all of his life. The vet thought he was three or four years old when we got him, although there was no way to be certain. He was missing teeth, had scars from several confrontations and had been beaten and abused. He was not much to look at, was short-tempered with Digger and constantly tried to assert himself as the alpha-male of the pack.

Larry took Jethro on and challenged his temperament, worked him and ran with him. Jethro put on weight and would eagerly work a trail. Jethro would trail, warbling and baying as he worked. He eventually developed chronic arthritis in his hips and when it was evident that the pain overrode the medication, he was euthanized. His heart and his drive on the trail will never be forgotten.

Ben, Ch. Questers Pursuit of Justice, and I are still working. He is three now and still knocks 'em dead in the show ring and bowls them over on the trail. Ben was a gift from Julie and Pat Cardinal. What a gift! He is a persistent worker who leans into the harness and does his best work in the crummiest circumstances. He has recovered evidence, human remains, lost children, hunters, and has done a wonderful job as a searcher.

The newest member of the household is Kailey, Ch. Legacy T-Bone Divine Comedy. She is every bit her name, an energetic, impatient comedian that loves the harness. Her training has been fun and exciting as I watch her absorb the training and enthusiastically take to the trail. She had major successes on the trail before she was seven months old. Her show championship was slower because she refuses to take anything, except trailing, seriously and loves to clown around in the ring. Kailey is a working dynamo!

Bloodhounds are consummate workers dedicated to the trail and their person. They reach deep into your heart and hang on, and they will richly reward the handler with dedication and love.

Ben.
Photo by Jan Tweedie

Introduction

People will get lost. It happens every day. They get lost in shopping malls, unfamiliar towns, parks, campgrounds, and wilderness areas. Getting lost is the easy part. People of all ages, races, creeds, and both sexes are candidates. More adults than children are subjects of wilderness searches but children are more commonly the subject of suburban searches. People who escape the stresses of the business and family worlds by taking off into the forest and natural quiet and enchantment of the outdoors are the source of most of the search and rescue calls.

The unfortunate person who becomes the subject of a search and rescue mission is usually the same person who said, "It will never happen to me." This same person often neglects to check weather forecasts and area maps, underestimates the time necessary to complete a hike, or overestimates his/her own abilities.

Mother Nature is a powerful and unforgiving force, and an inexperienced person is more likely to underestimate the potential hazards, venturing forth unprepared, carrying fewer emergency supplies and gear. Weather changes are sudden and unpredictable—a freak snowstorm could last for days. Without proper clothing and shelter, a stranded person will perish.

Complicating the hazards for the outdoor enthusiast are physical problems, mental health problems, emotional disturbances and equipment failures, which all add to the risk.

It may appear that experienced professional guides and recreationalists go to extremes to prepare for a trip or an adventure. However, let them be teachers for those "weekend warriors" that choose to just "rough it" without equipment, maps or information for the area they want to explore.

When people become lost, they are in serious trouble. Panic is a natural but debilitating feeling; it will cloud judgment, incapacitate decision-making abilities and may force the victim to flee and perhaps fall. Hypothermia, the abnormal lowering of the body core temperature, claims hundreds of lives every year. Hypothermia is caused by exposure to cold temperatures without adequate clothing or fuel to maintain sufficient energy levels to keep the body core warm.

Recreational equipment stores sell millions of dollars' worth of supplies and information every year. There are organized outdoor groups that represent every outdoor activity interest and newcomers should be urged to join a group of experienced enthusiasts instead of venturing out on their own.

Experience is not a guarantee of safety. Search and rescue groups in the Pacific Northwest donate tens of thousands of hours every year to search and rescue operations; many of those rescued have been hunting or hiking for years without incident.

The key to returning home safely is starting out safely. This means getting current maps of the area, packing for the weather predicted and for severe weather conditions like snow, heavy rain and wind. It also involves writing a detailed trip agenda and leaving it with someone dependable who will notify authorities if the recreationalist does not return as planned.

The most important thing to remember is to resist changing plans halfway through the trip. If you decide to stay out a couple of extra days and don't tell your contact people, they may contact authorities, believing you are lost or injured. A search and rescue effort is costly, but more importantly, while the teams are searching unnecessarily for you, someone else may be in dire need of assistance and have to wait.

Remember, if you do get lost, stay in one place. Search teams have spent hours following a lost and moving person. Staying in one place, preferably next to a large clearing, will increase your chances of being located.

People will continue to believe that getting lost or injured will never happen to them, but eventually the odds go against us. We cannot predict accidents nor accurately predict changing weather; what we *can* do is prepare. Good search and rescue teams train for searches on a regular basis and they respond when someone is reported lost; however, the primary responsibility for being found lies with the victim.

The Bloodhound's keen sense of smell is unequalled. His floppy ears help to channel the scent particles toward the nose, and the folds droping over his eyes protect them from weeds and brush during a search.

CHAPTER ONE

Thinking Ahead

Owning a search dog is a commitment for the life of the dog. Search dogs and handlers forge a strong partnership bond and become a team. The search dog depends on the handler for support, encouragement, food, companionship and training, and we depend on the dog to lead us to a lost, injured or deceased person. We expect the search dog to work in freezing weather, rough terrain, for hours on end, in confusion and in danger. They work even when their bodies are injured and they are exhausted.

A search dog does not fare well without training, practice and work. Likewise, a handler does not do well in the field if he doesn't train on a regular basis. The team must work and play together.

Obtaining, equipping and working a search dog is purely a volunteer endeavor. There are hundreds of people that get lost each year, and maybe one percent send in a donation to the organization. Most civilians don't understand that these dogs are not financially supported by anyone but the owner. But as awareness and education increase, search dogs are gaining the attention of agencies, media and organizations.

Search dogs have responded to such incidents as devastating earthquakes in Mexico City, Armenia and the Philippines; teams responded to San Salvador after the mud slides; and they routinely assist with inner-city disasters, wilderness searches, and criminal trails. Water search teams have advanced working methods which have led to the recovery of drowned victims that could not be seen.

Search and rescue coordination is the responsibility of the law enforcement agency with jurisdiction over the area in which the person was lost. Law enforcement personnel can sometimes be skeptical and difficult to convince, but it is helpful to remember that law enforcement officers are in the proof business. If searches can prove something, clearly and tangibly, then the method is much more likely to be accepted. Trying to convince someone that a dog is following an invisible trail, however real, is tough.

Communication between law enforcement agencies is often limited as well. For example, one agency may accept the work of a particular search dog team but not inform any other agency. The handler will often read or hear about incidents that may have turned out more favorably had dog teams been called, but unfortunately, the agency wasn't aware of them!

Educating agencies responsible for contacting SAR resources is one of the toughest but most important ongoing

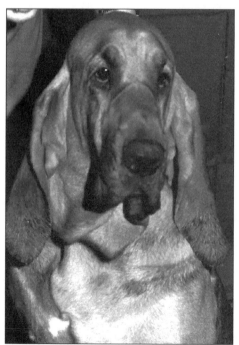

tasks of a search dog team. It is a delicate balance of phone calls, literature distribution and requests for demonstrations to achieve an atmosphere that is open to seeing the potential of a dog team.

The soft, engaging gaze of a Bloodhound is captivating.
PHOTO BY ANNE LEGGE

As teams develop, it is predictable that a certain competitiveness will arise whenever two groups of people are offering similar services. The key is to unite the two groups to form one powerful alliance dedicated to improving and advertising the SAR resource.

Once the team has been accepted by a community of agencies, there are times of pure boredom and other times of absolute exhaustion. Call-outs may come at any hour of any day and teams must be ready, willing and able to respond anywhere and at any time.

Bloodhound hugs are VERY important.
PHOTO BY JAN TWEEDIE

The agencies that use SAR dogs usually expect specific teams to respond to their calls and are slow to accept changes. I have worked the same two dogs for the past seven years and when I demonstrate a new pup, it is interesting to observe the skepticism that prevails until I harness the pup and he proves himself.

Whether handlers are actually in training or are contemplating working a search dog, it is important that they are aware of the time and money involved in this endeavor. Veterinary costs, equipment, and conditioning all play a dominant role in the normal maintenance of SAR dogs.

Training and searching with a dog is something that requires creative thinking and creative financing and many handlers are shocked at the amount of money that is needed to support their team for a year. Veterinary costs include routine immunizations, annual or semi-annual physicals for the dog and treatment of injuries and illnesses that may crop up.

Potential is evident at a very early age. PHOTO BY SCOTT McKIERNAN.

An average year of feed, equipment, shelter and travel for the average dog team can be more than $3,000. Add to that any additional training, out-of-area or out-of-state searches, or unexpected veterinary calls and costs continue to go up. International response requires additional money; a passport, travel and accommodations, veterinary exams, and pocket money will be needed. And don't forget that time off from a "regular job" adds up quickly. As handlers become more skilled they usually require more equipment; the costs keep adding up.

Exercise and physical conditioning for the handler is just as important as it is for the dog. Poor physical conditioning will contribute to more injuries and less stamina in the field. Walking, running, biking, hiking, and aerobic exercise are all excellent ways to keep in shape. Remember that once you leave that nice warm bed to respond to a SAR call-out, you may work for hours in freezing weather, covering many miles before daylight.

Handlers should stay in contact with their personal physician as well and it may be necessary to educate your doctor regarding the physical demands of search and rescue work. Some physicians will be happy to help you prepare an advanced first aid kit for the field.

Injuries and illness should be taken care of immediately by a professional. Both handler and dog require thorough physicals every year. Some search groups and agencies require a certificate of good health as well as the shot records for the dogs. Proper diet for both the handler and the dog are crucial. A work-

At five weeks, Dancer is eager to leave the nest and explore.
PHOTO BY JAN TWEEDIE

ing dog needs a higher number of calories per day and a balanced diet, which the cheaper brands of dog food do not provide. A working handler needs access to ready sources of energy and stamina afforded by a good diet.

When you first begin to train your dog the time commitment will be heavy. Daily and sometimes twice-a-day workouts are needed, especially if you are starting with a puppy. The dog's attention span and yours will be relatively short, but your expectations will be high. Keep the work sessions short and frequent with plenty of play and bonding time in between. Plan on training one hour a day, six days a week for the first month, then at least five hours per week after that. As the dog masters the training exercises, don't let up. Continue to challenge both the dog and yourself with obstacles to encourage the constant growth and development.

Equipment must be undamaged, clean and ready to go at all times. Dedicating space in the garage, house or somewhere clean and dry and keeping all gear packed and ready is imperative. Inspect your gear often for signs of wear and don't patch equipment you depend on; replace it. Handlers should be on the mailing list for outdoor suppliers and should keep up to date on the most recent equipment.

Ten-week-old Kady arrives.
PHOTO BY JAN TWEEDIE

Many of us have full time jobs in our "real" lives. Employers can be extremely reluctant to grant SAR handlers leave from work when the pager goes off. It is best to inform employers from the beginning and to try to work out an arrangement that gives you maximum freedom to respond in an emergency. Some employers have criteria to which the callout description must adhere; for example, one employer will allow the handler to respond to any search involving a child. Another employer may allow the employee to respond to criminal searches and a third employer may not allow the employee to leave regardless of whether the employee offers to take annual leave or not. Educate your employer! Post articles about the searches you have been on and write thank-you letters for any time off. I encourage you to find a workable plan instead of calling in sick from a search base. Deceitful behavior will not pay off in the long run.

Jonah was the indulgent "brother" to baby Ben. Search dogs should be well socialized and be able to get along with other dogs and people. Starting early helps.
PHOTO BY JAN TWEEDIE

SAR volunteers can work in their own state to get legislation that would recognize the SAR volunteer as an Emergency Services Worker. This entitles the volunteer to annual leave without using the employee's accrued annual leave. Using all vacation time on searches is a wonderful contribution; however, the mental and physical well-being of the searcher is often dependent on periodic "real" vacations as well.

Working a search dog is a tough way to perform a community service. It can be very rewarding to find a lost child but it can be equally depressing to recover someone who died. Good luck. I hope that this book will assist you in your endeavor to work a searching dog. It's worth it.

Ready to go trick or treating!
PHOTO COURTESY OF RAY AND KAY SCHMITT.

CHAPTER TWO

Getting Started

A PUPPY OR AN ADULT?

Which is better, a puppy or an adult? Both stages have advantages and disadvantages and each handler must define their needs before choosing.

When raising a puppy, training and partnership expectations can be established right in the beginning. Behavior patterns can be monitored and are relatively easily altered at this early stage. And for the novice handler, starting a puppy allows a joint learning curve phase in which the handler and the dog discover habits and behavior as a team.

Handlers may want to avoid the trials of training a puppy and choose instead to take on an older dog. Training an adult dog may be difficult but it is possible and there are definite advantages to this route. House training and pitiful cries in the night are things of the past and socialization behaviors have been established. The disadvantages are that the handler may not know how the dog was socialized or the history of previous treatment; training and behavior may be irreversible. Taking on an adult dog can also be a strain on the existing dogs at the home. Handlers must weigh the benefits and costs of taking on an additional dog or an adult dog.

Be cautious when taking on an adult dog. Find out as much information about the dog's past as possible. Find out where the dog came from and why the previous owner is giving the dog up. It is essential that all records, including working, training and health, accompany the dog to its new home.

If the adult dog is untrained for working it is best to start slowly and only increase the challenges as the dog becomes familiar with the expectations of the handler and the work routine. An adult dog may have an established working pattern, habits and alerting behavior to which the new owner must be sensitive. In my experience, an adult dog is more easily trained by an experienced handler with a lot of experience in training working dogs. I have had no problem with training adult dogs to work although the time commitment is much higher. Of the four Bloodhounds I started, two of the four were more than a year old at the onset of training.

The adult dog may have established habits and characteristics that are not conducive to working and this can be avoided by carefully evaluating the dog prior to placement. Behaviors such as digging, fence jumping, fence climbing, barking, aggressive behavior, biting, and aggression towards children or other dogs are usually very difficult to change. Do not, for any reason, take on an adult dog who is aggressive or has a record of attacks on other dogs or people. A biting dog is a liability.

Whether puppy or adult, once the dog is in your hands your dedication, training and consistency will determine the success or failure of the partnership.

STARTING YOUR SEARCH
FOR THE RIGHT PUPPY

When selecting your working dog as a puppy it is important for you to know as much as possible about the puppy's early life prior to your selection. Many breeders invite prospective buyers to visit the litter after the puppies are at least three weeks of age. In the first two to three weeks the puppies are very susceptible to illness and disease and should not be handled by outside people.

Talk with the breeder ahead of time and find out as much as possible about the sire and dam (father and mother) of the litter. While there have been terrific search dogs born to non-working parents, this information is helpful to determine the potential of the bloodline.

Talk with other handlers and look at a variety of dogs to determine the coloring, size, sex and type you are looking for. If you see an example of what you would like, talk with the owner. Find out the background and bloodline of the particular dog and contact the breeder to find out if there will be future puppies, costs and additional information about the prospective parents.

The price of puppies will vary greatly. A Bloodhound puppy ranges in price from $150 to over one thousand dollars. A trained dog, if you can find one for sale, may cost hundreds to thousands of dollars. But price does not guarantee anything. There are many dogs out there

Kailey at five weeks.
PHOTO BY HELEN RADCLIFFE

that cost five hundred to one thousand dollars as puppies and are not working as SAR dogs due to a lack of desire to work, poor physical structure, hip dysplasia, and a host of other problems.

There are breeders who produce excellent puppies but there are also breeders who produce poor quality puppies. Breeders who produce pups with physical problems, bad bites, structural faults, temperament problems, lack of desire to work, or general health problems should be avoided. Talk to other owners,

Kids and Bloodhounds — a natural mix.
PHOTO BY JAN TWEEDIE

breeders and handlers about reputable breeders before you invest a lot of money.

I do not recommend buying dogs from pet stores or retail outlets. Their suppliers are, traditionally, "puppy mills," people who breed dogs for money. They sell the puppies to "brokers" who in turn sell the puppies to pet stores and retail outlets. "Puppy mills" produce poor quality puppies that often have a host of medical and temperamental problems.

There are several ways to select a puppy. Some breeders select the puppy for the buyer based on an application or interview where the buyer is asked a variety of questions. Distant buyers who are unable to physically observe the litter should be sent photographs or videos of all the puppies, as well as of the puppy selected for them and of the sire and dam of the litter. New photos of the puppies should be taken weekly and a copy sent to the anxious buyers so that they can keep track of their puppy's growth.

Another method of choosing a puppy involves spending some time with the puppies which meet your specified criteria and selecting one from that group.

A third method is allowing the puppy to choose you. When the buyer plays with the pups, most of them will usually quickly lose interest except for perhaps one or two puppies that will remain with you. Make your selection from them.

There are still other, more informed buyers who gather information on the sire and dam, closely examine the temperament and trailing test results and observe the litter before making the final selection. Some buyers prefer to specify a specific sex, coloring, or purpose for the dog and allow the breeder

Even as tiny puppies the trademark extra skin is evident.
PHOTO BY JAN TWEEDIE

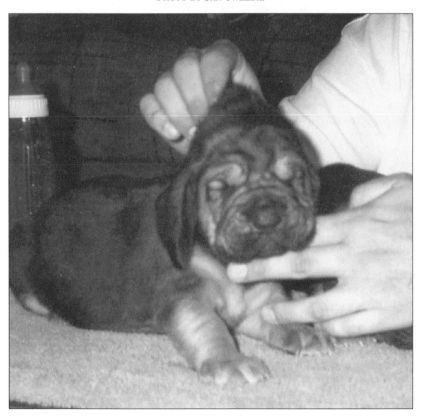

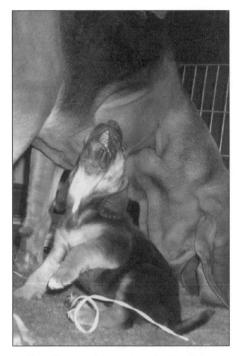

Ben thoroughly enjoys babysitting and teaching the babies to search.
PHOTO BY JAN TWEEDIE

to segregate those puppies that appear to meet these criteria—the buyer then chooses from that group. Since all puppies tend to be adorable and hard to resist, this may be the best method for you. Good breeders spend a great deal of time with the litter, from birth until the pups leave for new homes. Thus the breeder may be the best one to make the selection.

In the first litter of puppies we produced I encouraged buyers to choose their own puppy from "criteria" groups. That means puppies are grouped according to temperament, working ability, and structural quality. This system worked marginally well, but later I wished I had done more of the matching. In subsequent litters we matched buyer with puppy depending on the desires of the buyer. So far each of those matches has worked out well.

PUPPY SELECTION AND TESTING

Once you have narrowed your search to a particular litter, there are several simple tests you can perform to help you make your final selection. Evaluating puppies for temperament and scenting ability should be done early in the puppy's life. Breeders must pay attention to the activities of the puppies and many breeders will keep detailed development records.

Puppies should be evaluated continually throughout puppy-hood. The best time for specific testing is at four weeks of age to determine the obvious trailers from those more easily distracted. Temperament testing is equally as important and must be done between the 48th and 50th day of life.

Breeders should watch for aggression, independence, fear, agitation and growth patterns. Most breeders that work search dogs will categorize the puppies as they grow.

TEMPERAMENT TESTING

Temperament testing is not a lifelong guarantee because the development of the individual temperament will be influenced by its living situation and handler temperament. However, temperament testing will indicate training potential and level of dependence in puppies and is usually a good indicator of the baseline behavior that can be expected of the dog as it grows and matures.

Temperament testing should occur in a quiet spot away from the puppy's normal habitat. If the puppies are kept inside the house, temperament testing should be done in the garage, yard or another location which is foreign to the puppy. A change in the floor surface is recommended.

Puppies should be grouped together and removed from the group one at a time. The waiting and finished puppies should be out of earshot of the testing area.

Temperament testing requires an extra person who is familiar with the testing process but who is not familiar to the puppies. Temperament testing includes evaluating how the puppy acclimates to a strange environment, the puppy's resistance to control, interest in retrieving a sock or a ball, the puppy's startle reflex and recovery from it, whether the puppy will follow you or not, and how the puppy responds to being petted and touched.

Another test involves walking the puppy across a foreign surface such as plastic tarp, grate or fencing material lying on the ground, which tests the puppy's willingness to adapt to a strange environment.

Dog temperament is critical. Digger and Melvin worked together,
napped together, and shared human friends totally.
PHOTO BY JAN TWEEDIE

There are a number of publications which address puppy temperament testing. The six tests that are used can be found in detail in a variety of breed-specific and general-interest books that are currently on the market.

TRAILING TESTING

Testing for trailing ability is more difficult and depending on the rater, the results may vary. The scored results will define the potential trailing puppies. Puppies should be tested between the fourth and fifth week of life. Optimal testing conditions exist when the puppies are hungry; hunger encourages the puppy to work harder to receive the food reward.

You can perform this test with one puppy or with as many as three pups at a time. The test will require a crate (or box large enough to hold the puppies), a fifty-foot tape measure, a fifty-foot section of rope or twine, food reward, paper, pencil and a stopwatch.

The area for the trailing test should be outside; grassy areas are excellent. It is best if the puppies are not familiar with the testing area because the new smells and sounds will be useful in the test.

Place the pups in the crate and prop the door closed with a stick attached to the twine or rope. Make sure that a jerk on the twine will open the door and release the puppies. Show the food reward to the pups in the crate, encouraging and teasing them with the food reward. Start backing away from the crate, talking to the puppies as you back away to reassure them.

Spilling some of the food reward about four feet in front of the crate gives the puppies a direction of travel. Some handlers continue to bait the puppies every few feet to the end of the twine while other handlers leave a shirt or jacket halfway down the line from which the puppies can work. Other handlers leave nothing along the path, go to the end of the string, pop the crate open, lie down and wait.

Lie down on the ground and remain still, without making any noise. Pull the twine to release the door and start the stop-watch. Watch the individual puppies as they leave the crate and look for the puppies that immediately put their nose down and begin working towards you. As the puppies reach the spilled food, watch for the puppies that locate the spill and immediately continue working towards you. Record the time that each puppy takes getting from the crate to you and the food bowl.

Some raters will place the food out of sight behind them and continue to run the time until the puppies locate the food dish. Remember, the puppies are looking for the food, which is the actual article you gave them to smell.

In some litter testing I have not used food at all. Using a person that is very familiar to the puppies as the search goal will provide the same information. Use a well-worn piece of that person's clothing and use it instead of the food tease. Drag the item along the ground from the front of the crate to a distance of about six feet from the crate. Lift the item up and drop and drag it every six feet or so to the end of the twine. Release the puppies, time their approach and record their responses to the scent and following it to its source.

A puppy that wanders around the crate whining or crying or a puppy that refuses to search for the food or the person, sitting down or wandering off in the wrong direction, should be tested again under the same circumstances the next day. If the

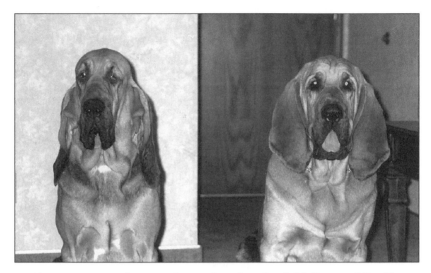

Dogs must get along on the road and in the field. Ben and Truffle shared motel rooms on the show circuit.
PHOTO BY SUZI PAINE

behavior is repeated, that particular pup is either not a potential working dog or else it will require a lot of patient training, possibly exhibiting very minimal skills.

BRINGING YOUR PUPPY HOME

Once you have selected your puppy, your next task is to attend to the paperwork involved with the purchase and arrange to get him home. I release puppies at nine to ten weeks of age or after the first series of worming and shots. Puppies should not be released to new homes during the eighth week as there has been research to show that puppy temperament is extremely fragile during this week; the puppy may be vulnerable to fears and bad experiences which can stay with them for life. Be wary of someone who will let you take a puppy before it is six weeks old.

Buyers should determine whether they will pick the puppy up or have the puppy shipped. Puppies should not be shipped prior to ten weeks of age. Be sure that the puppy is shipped on a direct flight to avoid delays or loss. The less bumping and noise to which the puppy is subjected the better. Choose the flight that is most direct and quickest, *not* the cheapest.

Buyers should be given the puppy's complete health record upon receipt, including a growth chart with weights at weekly intervals, worming evaluation, medication, and shot record. If dew claws were removed or if the puppy received treatment for any reason, that information should be included in the health record as well. If the buyer has any questions, the name, address and phone number of the breeder's veterinarian should be included in the health record.

In any puppy, particularly a shipped puppy, the breeder and buyer should agree in advance that the buyer is to have the puppy examined at the buyer's veterinarian (and at the buyer's expense) within forty-eight hours of receiving the puppy. If there is a problem with which the buyer can't or won't deal, the puppy can immediately be returned to the breeder (at the buyer's expense). Most reputable breeders will encourage this veterinary examination and will welcome a copy of the first examination paperwork.

QUESTIONS FOR SELLERS TO ASK POTENTIAL BUYERS

1. Have you ever owned this breed before? If yes, what happened to the other dog(s)? If not, why did you choose this breed?
2. Have you ever owned a large dog before?
3. Do you have a fenced yard or kennel enclosure? If so, how big? If not, how will you confine him?
4. Are you aware that this breed requires exercise?
5. What are your methods for disciplining a puppy?
6. Do you have a veterinarian?
7. What do you plan to do with the dog? If work, how do you plan to train? If show, are you going to take lessons?
8. Do you have any other dogs at this time? If so, how will you make sure that the dogs get along? How will you introduce them? Are they the same sex? What about breeding?
9. Are you aware that these dogs slobber quite a bit?
10. How did you hear of this litter?

QUESTIONS THE BUYER SHOULD ASK THE SELLER

Buyers who are up-front and gather information regarding the breeder, sir and dam and the litter prior to buying are much better prepared than the impulse buyer. Remember that you are making a commitment for the life of the dog.

1. Are both the sire and dam located on the breeder's premises? If yes, ask to see both. Check for temperament and general physical condition. If not, are there pictures available? Where is the dam? Why?
2. Have the puppies been temperament tested? If yes, by whom, how and what were the results on the litter?
3. Is a pedigree available?
4. Do the sire and dam work or show? If yes, have they finished championships? What is their working reputation? Get references.
5. Have the puppies received their first shots?
6. Has the litter been wormed?
7. Has the litter been examined by a veterinarian? Get the name and phone number of the vet and get copies of the records.
8. Is the breeder willing to be contacted for training or follow-up?
9. Is the kennel area clean?
10. Do the puppies seem active and in good health?
11. Have the show quality puppies been evaluated for conformation to the breed standard? If so, who evaluated them? What was the result?
12. Have the working quality puppies been evaluated? If so, who evaluated them and what was the result?
13. Has the breeder had a litter before? If so, ask for the names of some of the buyers.
14. Has the litter been registered?
15. Will the puppy be required to carry the breeder's kennel name?
16. Will the breeder assign a name to the puppy?
17. Will the breeder replace the puppy or refund the price if a genetic health problem is discovered?
18. Will the breeder guarantee show quality after reasonable effort?

Buyers must be curious and ask questions. Remember that although the breeder may have a long list of accomplishments and titles, the buyer is making a significant investment of both time and money during the lifetime of the dog. Make your decisions wisely.

If you are purchasing a registered puppy (purebred, registered with the American Kennel Club) the papers should be shipped with the puppy if the purchase price and the shipping costs have been paid.

When purchasing a puppy there are a number of things you should receive in addition to the puppy. You should be given the health record, pedigree and registration papers or registration information with the litter or individual registration number. You should also get the results of temperament testing and trailing testing. A responsible breeder will also give you a suggested diet and basic information about the litter and specific information regarding follow-up immunizations and care.

Puppy selection can be simple and done quickly or it can be a well-informed decision. Remember that all puppies are adorable and hard to pass up. Make your decision wisely and it will pay off for you *if* you follow through with the time and training required.

HIRING A TRAINER OR BUYING A TRAINED DOG

I have been asked by new handlers a number of times to take a puppy and train it to search. I always refuse. I have *assisted* a number of new handlers in training their dogs and have trained new *handlers*, but I don't believe that someone can train your dog to search for you. A paid trainer should be consistent with exercise sessions, training goals and objectives as well as with practical handler training. You should be the primary handler during all classes and exercises. There is no set minimum or maximum hours that it takes to train a dog to be field-ready. Make sure that the agreement you enter into has specific parameters defining your financial commitment as well as the time and task commitment made by the trainer.

The most critical time in building a partnership with a search dog is in the initial training period while both the handler and the dog are learning the ropes. Important training takes place as the handler observes behavior indicating an alert and other trail signals.

Choosing a kennel name to mark your particular Bloodhounds is fun.
Ray and Kay Schmitt chose Maple Hill Kennels.
PHOTO BY KAY SCHMITT

There are some dogs that are trained and handled by more than one person and are termed "multi-handler" dogs. Usually the primary handler is the one who does the basic training, and the extra handlers are added once the dog is trained. It is imperative that the person who will be the primary handler in the field is the person who handles the dog in the primary stages of training. It is the handler's responsibility to know the methods and abilities of the dog.

Occasionally a trained dog is available for placement into a new home when the original handler is unable to retain the dog for some reason. It is best to visit the dog and work with the handler prior to removing the dog from its home. I highly recommend that the training and working records of the dog accompany the dog to its new location so that the new handler is aware of the dog's strengths and weaknesses. Not only does this give the new handler an idea of the training the dog has experienced, it also prevents the dog from getting bored through redundant training techniques.

In some cases a trained dog will be put up for sale. This can occur for a variety of reasons but be cautious of purchasing trained dogs. Before purchasing a "trained" dog, find out what the past training included. Was the dog trained for working wilderness, evidence, or cadaver searches? Who trained the dog and how was it trained? Are there written training records? Why is the dog posted for sale?

I have come across very few well-trained dogs that were for sale. Often the dog advertised as "trained" has received very little training in anything more than basic behavior and often was barely introduced to field search training.

Most handlers that put the time into training a dog will not sell it except in rare circumstances. More often these dogs are placed with friends or family or returned to the breeder to place. These handlers are more interested in ensuring that the dog will be cared for and worked than they are in financial gain. Ask plenty of questions before seriously considering this option and consult with other handlers who know the dog and the owner before purchasing.

Training your own dog is the best method there is to establish the partnership that will be crucial in the field. Asking for or receiving assistance in training your dog is certainly acceptable and encouraged. The goal is to build a strong foundation of trust and skills to bring into an emergency search and rescue operation.

"Teething."
BY CRYSTAL MELVIN

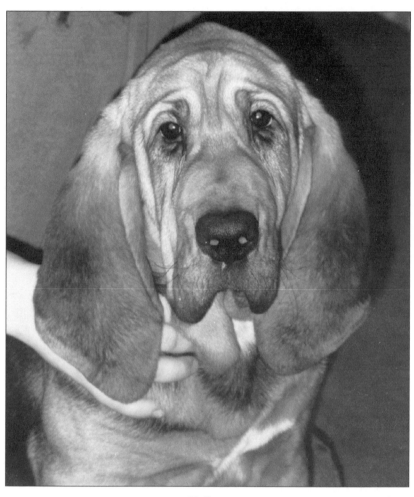

Kailey.
PHOTO BY JAN TWEEDIE

CHAPTER THREE

Training Basics

T his section is dedicated to an overview of training and gives some examples of training schedules, progression schedules and handler training information. Specific types of training will be covered in detail but keep in mind that it is important to develop a training schedule that includes new skills as well as a solid review of mastered skills.

HANDLER TEMPERAMENT

Not everyone should be a dog owner and not every dog owner should be a dog handler. It takes a special temperament to raise, train and work a dog. The time and effort involved in training a working dog are endless.

A dog is naturally curious and can be frightened by new or strange things. It is the handler's responsibility to set limits, to establish rules and expectations for the dog and to introduce new things slowly and without pressure.

During training it is important to expose the dog to as many new smells and sights as possible, with each new situation carefully and slowly introduced. Rushing the dog or punishing it for cowering away from a strange situation, person, animal or noise will reinforce the instinctual "fight or flight" response to a threat. Patrick, a friend of mine, was training his first Bloodhound, Tory. They were training in a pasture near their home and the trail they were working went right past a herd of cows. Tory didn't know what those beasts were and so she cowered, bayed and promptly hid behind Patrick, losing all interest in the trail.

Patrick tried dragging Tory up to one of the cows but Tory would not have it. She bucked and wailed and bolted. Patrick grew frustrated and angry because Tory was afraid and couldn't, or wouldn't, trail past them. He tried sweet–talking her, then a matter–of–fact approach and finally, in exasperation, he ordered and demanded her to get through it. None of it worked.

Over time Tory seems to have figured out what those huge animals are and that they mean her no harm. Patrick made sure that she had plenty of exposure to them and as a result she seems to have overcome her fear of cows. For quite some time Patrick made sure there were trails laid through pastures, making sure the cows crossed the runners' trails, forcing Tory to work past them to reach her goal. Tory pays little or no attention to livestock anymore.

Everyone gets frustrated in different situations. Dogs can become frustrated, too, when handlers demand too much too fast; they become confused. Abusive handling not only is ineffective, it is the quickest way for a dog to learn to mistrust the handler.

Psychological punishment is as hard on any dog as physical punishment. Yelling at the dog should be a clear indicator that *you* did something wrong. Shouting is a sure sign that *you* are frustrated and that the training session should stop immediately. When you are angry your frustrations are passed directly down the lead to the dog. Notice your body posture. You may be leaning slightly forward, hands clenched into fists, your jaw may be tight and the lead is taut. Stop right there. Leave the dog alone until you have regained your composure. Review the training session and locate the point at which you became frustrated. That point will indicate where additional training is needed.

Some handlers take everything personally, as a personal insult if their dog did not make the find or perform to their expectations. Search and rescue work is not a game of winning and losing. The goal is for *someone* to find the missing person or article. It matters only that the person is found, not who

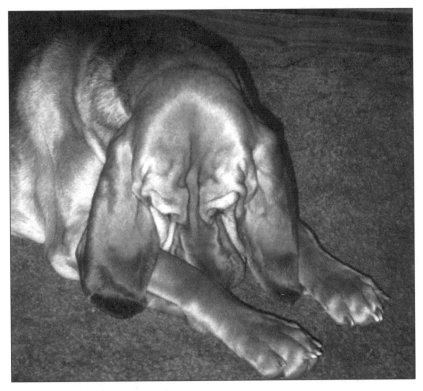

A scolding brings about instant sadness. Ben asking for forgiveness after getting caught stealing cookies from Kady.
PHOTO BY JAN TWEEDIE

finds him. Handling a dog in a search and rescue situation, or in any working situation, is a process of teamwork with other dogs, handlers and search teams.

At a search base a few years ago, I walked up on a dog handler screaming at his dog and hitting him because someone else's dog had found the missing person. I immediately got angry. I walked up to the handler and told him to quit hitting the dog. I asked the handler what had happened.

This was the handler's fourth search and he had worked hard to become qualified. The handler said that the dog hadn't really worked very hard and was not near the area where the person was found. In fact the person was found in another

Through brush and thick cover . . .

To the happy ending — A FIND!
Photos by Kay Schmitt

area. Then the handler said, in a quiet voice, that he himself had chosen the area they worked. The handler was wrong and took his frustrations out on the dog. The handler continued to search in other missions with his dog. I never saw him raise his voice to the dog again. They have done well in the field, making several finds.

I also confronted another handler by telling him to stop hitting his dog. The handler stood up and yelled that he knew his own dog and that the dog had failed. He then said that the dog should have been able to air scent the missing person who had been found lying in a canyon over a steep ridge from where the dog was working. I told the handler that I didn't think beating the dog was any way to treat a partner, and he told me to leave him alone and that he knew how to handle the problem. He ordered the dog into his car. The dog cowered at his feet and licked his boot. The handler kicked the dog and stomped off in frustration. This handler was someone who had no business working a dog, because he simply did not have the right temperament. Fortunately, this handler is no longer involved in search and rescue work.

If you physically punish the dog in a moment of anger you risk losing the dog's confidence and trust. Clearly setting the rules and enforcing them on a regular basis with praise for compliance is much easier for the dog to understand. A person who feels compelled to hit or kick or physically abuse a dog because the dog didn't make a find or missed a turn reflects not a bad dog but the need for additional training and should make you stop and think.

There are a number of handlers who are very good at what they do and have been doing it for years. These handlers build success into every part of their training programs. You cannot become an expert overnight, nor will your dog make a find every time you are called out. It just doesn't happen. You may have the good fortune to make great progress and do excellent work early in your training. Just remember to pace yourself. Take the training one day at time and encourage the dog to work with you. Be patient.

Setting clear rules and consistently reinforcing the dog with praise for good behavior is much easier for a dog to

---

RULES FOR WORKING AND TRAINING DOGS

1. Searches are not always successful.
2. A dog's behavior will not always be consistent.
3. There will be times that the dog will not perform to your expectation.
4. Search and rescue operations are not competitions—the goal is to find the victim.
5. Abusing the dog will only escalate the behavior you are trying to stop. This includes physical and verbal abuse.
6. Dogs must be worked patiently and consistently, with praise for every success.
7. If you become frustrated, stop the training exercise and resume when you feel calm. Remember, it is not the dog's fault.
8. Spend time relaxing and playing with the dog outside of the training time.
9. Introduce new concepts to the dog gradually.

---

understand. Train one day at a time and encourage the dog to work *with* you. Watch yourself for signs of frustration. Make lessons simple and clear and review training daily to identify areas that need more work. Set attainable goals for the team and remember that working a dog is not a competition, it is a skill and a partnership.

DOG TEMPERAMENT

Search dogs have been traditionally considered friendly and outgoing since they search for strangers all the time. An aggressive or unfriendly search dog is ineffective as well as a liability and should not be worked. Biting, lunging and growling are all examples of inappropriate behavior. Dogs react toward people based on perceived threats, fearing that they or the handler will be hurt. It is helpful to understand this instinctual behavior when you are teaching the dog acceptable behavior.

Applying a muzzle is not the answer nor is locking the dog up. Careful and patient training will stop undesirable behavior in most dogs. Unacceptable behavior can be viewed as a natural fear that has gotten out of control. The handler that strikes or yells at the dog for this activity is reinforcing the fear. Work slowly and firmly. If the dog continues the behavior it should be removed from the field and not be allowed around *anyone* other than the handler. The vehicle should be marked with warning signs and the dog should never be left unattended or unsecured.

There are several Bloodhounds I have come across that have temperament problems. They bite, lunge and growl. In several cases the handlers tie the dogs to their vehicles and walk away. Oftentimes the handler is out of sight of the dog and therefore unable to watch for situations where the dog might get into trouble. Even though the handlers' own organization constantly reminds them, they continue to leave the dogs unattended, even in public areas where children or adults might approach the "cute doggy."

A law enforcement canine is taught to protect the handler and the handler's property, but a search dog that is not working as an aggression dog should not be taught aggression or protection and should be discouraged from exhibiting these characteristics.

A dog that attacks or attempts to attack other dogs should be trained to accept other dogs. Because of transportation logistics at search bases it is often necessary to transport more than one dog in a vehicle. If you have to drive your own vehicle or if your dog requires special handling and a separate vehicle, the chances of being called out on wilderness searches requiring limited vehicles will diminish.

Start socializing your dog when he is young. Have him ride, play and work with other pups. Digger, at twelve years old, gladly jumped into any vehicle and rode with any dog as long as the dog wasn't aggressive. Even when jumped, Digger's instinct was to put me between him and the ill-mannered dog and forget about him.

Make sure that you introduce strange dogs to each other on neutral ground. Often a fight will erupt when you bring a strange dog into another dog's turf. Put collars and leads on

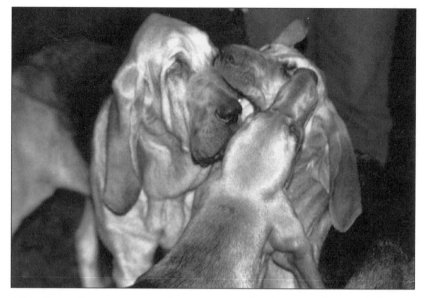

Bloodhounds are very social creatures and enjoy wrestling and playing together. Photo by Jan Tweedie

the dogs and walk them around the block and let them meet at a schoolyard or in the street. Once they get along, slowly and carefully bring them together on one another's territory. I do not advocate leaving two strange dogs alone for any reason; even dogs that are familiar with each other can erupt into a fight without warning. Supervise them at all times.

The dogs are exposed to other dogs at dog shows, trailing events, public appearances, and throughout training. I take my dogs to schools, through neighborhoods and to visit hospitals and nursing homes. When a friend goes out of town their dog often comes to stay with us. My dogs are therefore accustomed to having their search dog counterparts over for playtime and sleepovers.

At feeding time it is important to emphasize separateness. I do not believe in making dogs compete for food. Each dog needs to know that he will get his dinner in his dish in his spot, wherever that may be. The dogs should not be allowed to eat the other dogs' food nor should they be allowed to hang out next to one of the other dogs that is still eating. Each dog gets his biscuit or treat each night at bedtime without fear that one of the others will steal it. The toy box is full of toys, and many are duplicates such as chewies and plush toys so that there is less chance of conflict.

Train the dog to do what you want through exposure, patience and reassurance, and reward good behavior. Work slowly through problem areas and refresh the dog's mind from time to time even when you are convinced the problem has ended.

EQUIPMENT

Before training, familiarize yourself with the equipment you will need and select equipment that will promote the progress and success of your team. Handling equipment can be expensive, so choose wisely.

Equipment should be selected for its durability and ease of operation. Nylon webbing has replaced leather for almost all dog equipment. It is machine washable, easy to repair and does not stretch or break under stress. Leather will wear and crack in adverse weather and requires regular maintenance. The longevity and durability of the equipment you purchase should be a major factor in your choices.

There are several groups of equipment to consider. Some of the equipment is determined by the type of search dog you will be working. If the dog is going to be handled on-lead and in-harness, you will need a durable lead and harness combination as well as other equipment. Basic feeding and housing equipment will be the same for either an on-lead or off-lead dog, as are veterinary care and first aid supplies.

HOUSING

If you want the dog to live outdoors, house the puppy or dog outdoors from the start. I usually have a new puppy in the house with me for the first night or two, but during the day the puppy is outside in his yard to help him acclimate. The puppy yard has a big play area that is twelve feet wide and thirty feet long. The puppy has access to a snug dog house and a number of puppy toys for teething and recreation. There is a radio playing

Working gear must be in top condition.
PHOTO BY JAN TWEEDIE

at all times inside the dog house so that noise, talk and music can comfort him should he feel lonely.

Puppies can be very manipulative and will cry during the night if they are lonely or bored. This is where toys, chewies and the radio can help you. Be sure that the toys and chewies you give him are safe for him to eat and play with. Once the puppy knows that you are not going to rescue him every time he cries he will seek out other ways of entertaining himself or he will curl up and sleep. Be stoic and firm but remember to reinforce good behavior.

A puppy raised indoors acclimates to the indoor temperatures and conditions. If you live in a climate that gets snow and low temperatures in the winter it is important that your dog be acclimated to working in such weather. Housing the dog outside, year–round, keeps the dog acclimated as the seasons and temperatures change. Some handlers keep the dog in the house or garage at night but during the day the dog stays outside. This arrangement also helps to acclimate the dog.

If the dog is going to sleep, play and live outside, a secure area and a warm dog house are critical. A Bloodhound that runs loose is a dead dog. Dog waste, tipped over garbage cans, cars, chemicals, and a host of other hazards follow the loose dog. Be forewarned that puppies may not be sold unless a fenced, secure yard is available.

A dog on a chain is similarly at risk. The dog can hang himself, break the chain and get loose or wind the chain around the post so tightly that it can't move or access food and water. It can also become a target for cruel children and adults who might tease or taunt it.

I built a six–foot chain link fence all the way around my backyard, and the dog yard is a 12' x 62' area fenced with six–foot chain link anchored in concrete. Be sure the area you choose is "dog proof" and make sure that the dogs can't get under the fence. I use eight–foot landscaping timbers wedged under the bottom rail of the chain link fence to provide that extra security. Some handlers bury wire fencing underground to thwart diggers. Others use electric fences to prevent digging or escape. Make sure your fence is secure.

Add to your supplies a rubber water bucket for the back-yard. I recommend rubber horse buckets, which can be purchased at feed and livestock supply stores. Although water may freeze in it, the bucket itself will not freeze and you can just tip the bucket over and slide the frozen water block out. Metal and hard plastic buckets will freeze solid. If you use an ax or wreck-ing bar to break the ice out of your water buckets you will prob-ably end up splitting or punching holes in your buckets. Metal buckets may also freeze and split along the seams leaving sharp edges which can cause injury.

I choose to bed my dogs in hay or cedar chips. Use good quality timothy or alfalfa hay. They love to chew on the hay. Some handlers choose straw for bedding, because the hollow straw tubes provide insulation.

TRAINING EQUIPMENT

I never leave metal chain collars on a dog. I use a one–inch nylon web "semi-choke" collar that I make myself. The collar is designed to tighten only to a certain point and prevents the possibility of the dog hanging or choking himself. Be sure that you attach identification, rabies and license tags to collars if your local laws require them. To prevent rattling tags try using a rubber band to bind the tags tightly together.

Before putting a puppy out on his own, remove the collar to make sure that he doesn't work it partially over his head. A collar should be snug but you should be able to insert one finger sideways between the neck of the dog and the collar.

During searches I use a metal working collar or "choke" chain that is long enough (34 inches) to go around a dog's neck and secure back to the D-ring on the harness without putting pressure on his neck. This ensures that should he break the harness or should the harness have to be removed, I will still have control of the dog. The metal working collar is a signal to my dog that it's time to work—as soon as the lead is moved to the harness he knows that it's his turn to lead me and off we go!

It is handy to have a variety of leads from which to choose. I use an eighteen–inch "traffic lead" for loading and unloading, taking dogs in and out of buildings, through crowds and at demonstrations. I also use this short lead at the veterinarian's office to keep the dog close and out of harm's way.

A 4'-6' lead is excellent for walking the dog and for using on criminal searches. I also use the six–foot lead for working in heavy traffic. The working lead for the field ranges from 15'-20' long. I normally use a fifteen–foot lead on most searches. The twenty–foot lead is used on searches in open country and along bodies of water where there is little vegetation or timber in which to get tangled. Leads more than twenty feet long give the dog too much of a lead for the handler to have to deal with in brush or dense vegetation, and in criminal searches I want to keep the dog close to protect him.

The harness you use in the field must be durable and washable. After trying a variety of different kinds of harnesses including pulling harnesses, figure–8 harnesses and carting harnesses, I chose to modify and design one that maximized fluid movement and minimized points of binding or chafing. I chose nylon webbing used in mountain-climbing harnesses and rigging that is 1½ inches wide and has a stress load of at least two thousand pounds. The webbing is machine washable and easily sewn on the standard sewing machine.

In conjunction with a friend, I started a business called Big Red Search Supplies, making harnesses, collars and leads for working dogs. We also make radio harnesses for handlers to wear that fit on the handler's chest, making the radio much more accessible.

The harness I use has plastic, high-impact, quick–release buckles and is padded at the stress points on the chest, where the lead snaps in and on the side. The harnesses are designed to prevent the dog from backing out of the equipment and to place the pulling stress equally along the dog instead of concentrating it on the neck or back. The lead snaps onto a D-ring placed in the center of the back.

By the time my puppies are three weeks old they have felt the weight of a harness. By the time they are four weeks old they are comfortable with leads, collars and harnesses. The puppy harnesses we make are adjustable and are made from half–inch webbing.

Many handlers spend a great deal of time and thought on the color of their equipment. The colors usually vary with the searching activities; search and rescue equipment is often bright orange, bright yellow, bright blue and neon colors for heightened visibility. If you are planning to work in search and rescue it would be a good idea to have the bright colors. If you plan to work criminal cases I suggest you have equipment that is black or subdued in color to minimize visual exposure.

If you can't find equipment that you like, ask around. Talk to handlers that have the background and who may have the experience to make the items. Many of them probably manufacture some of their own equipment. There will be a substantial financial investment in equipment for both you and your dog, but it is worth it to select high–quality, durable equipment that will last and enhance your response, not hold you up or break down.

PACKING FOR A MISSION

The easiest way to transport all of your equipment is to place the dog's working gear into a nylon duffel bag. Duffel bags are usually made of nylon material and are lightweight as well as washable. They are usually inexpensive and readily available. I recommend using one bag per dog.

The duffel bags that I use are approximately twenty–four inches long and have a zipper all the way across the top of the bag. One bag contains a primary and a backup harness (different colors), a primary and backup lead (different colors), a backup working collar, a collapsible water bucket, two self-sealing plastic bags, each containing one meal for the dog (including vitamins), two pairs of working gloves (primary and backup), extra headlamp batteries, six gallon-sized scent article bags, two unused paper sacks, a canine first aid kit, a stainless steel food dish, and treats for the dog, such as jerky or freeze–dried liver. All of the items can be nested together in the bag. In addition to these supplies, carry one wool blanket in the back of the car and a few old towels for drying both you and the dog.

I choose a different color bag for each dog so that I know the proper harness, lead, collar and gear is in the bag I grab. It's best to have one harness for each dog adjusted and ready to go at all times. Always have backup collars and harnesses in the car and preferably one backup lead in case of breakage or loss. I have an "extras" duffel with two adjustable harnesses, spare gloves, two spare leads, two collars, and treats. It stays in my patrol car at all times and I have an identical bag in my personal vehicle.

MAINTAINING YOUR EQUIPMENT

After every mission in which the gear is used, I check it over. I look for damage and wear, and send it through the washer when needed. Make sure that your gear is clean and in excellent condition at all times. If you launder your gear make sure that you wash only one harness at a time so that in the event of a call-out you can respond with dry gear!

Webbing and nylon material should be washed whenever it becomes dirty, oily or has been exposed to chemicals or weather. Place leads and harnesses in a pillowcase and tie the case shut or place the items in a small duffel bag and put it in the washer. Bagging the items prevents them from wrapping around the agitator in your washer. Wash in cold water on a gentle cycle. You may want to pre-soak your gear if it is heavily soiled. After washing, hang the items to dry or tumble dry on a low temperature. Be sure you leave the leads in a pillowcase if you dry them in the dryer. The metal snaps can chip or damage the drum as they dry. Do not bleach your web gear as it may weaken the material. Sewing machines that are equipped with a leather or heavy denim needle can be used for creating or repairing your equipment. Some shoe and boot repair shops will stitch these items for you at a nominal cost.

EQUIPMENT FOR YOU

Your personal search and rescue equipment must include shelter, food, clothing and foul weather gear. I strongly urge you to include a good sleeping bag filled with either down or *Hollofil* which will keep you warm when the temperature dips below freezing. Most sleeping bags carry a temperature designation, so look for a bag that will keep you warm at zero degrees.

Make sure the sleeping bag has a waterproof "stuff sack" to carry it in but hang it up in storage when not in use to allow the loft to remain expanded, which will keep you warmer. Most searchers also invest in a good sleeping pad. There are a number of items on the market ranging from closed-cell foam to self-inflating mattresses. Camping supply stores, military surplus and commercial outfitter supply stores carry these items.

A lightweight, two-person tent is an excellent investment. They are large enough to accommodate both the dog, if so desired, and the handler or will accommodate two large adults and quite a lot of gear. Some searchers carry an emergency shelter such as a tube tent in their daypack. This is a highly recommended addition to your survival pack.

Although most search base camps provide food for the search teams, there will be times that you will need to prepare your own food in the field. Include a well-built and lightweight stove, fuel, and one cooking pot for preparing meals. You will need more than cold food to sustain your stamina and energy levels. Be prepared to cook for yourself as well as your dog on all call–outs. Plan ahead and bring high-calorie, nutritious food and leave it at the base camp so that it will be available. Remember to carry at least one meal for your dog in your day pack in the field.

There is a comprehensive list of required equipment at the end of this section. You may want to add to the equipment suggested as you define your personal equipment needs. Always be prepared to spend the night out in the elements. Planning to search during daylight hours only and retiring to an area motel is not realistic nor feasible on most searches.

Food items should be lightweight and require a minimum of preparation time. Military MRE's (Meals Ready to Eat) make excellent pack food although they may be hard to find. Military surplus stores and some catalogs and outfitter outlets carry them. The advantage of the MRE's is that the envelope includes a main dish, fruit or dessert, snack, utensils, gum and toilet paper. They can be eaten unheated or submerged in boiling water for a few minutes. Dehydrated foods and pre-packaged, pre-cooked meals are fine. Be sure that whatever food you choose to carry is lightweight and can be heated to provide a hot meal.

Liquids are an important part of your food cache. Include hot beverages such as cocoa, coffee or tea as well as pre-sweetened cold beverages like lemonade or an electrolyte replacer such as *Gatorade, Powerburst,* or *Sports Drink.*

You will want to invest in a couple of items for transporting your equipment; a sturdy daypack with outside pockets big enough to hold plastic water bottles (I use the same type of bottles as the professional bicycle racers) is useful. A daypack will cost between $15 and $100 depending on how fancy you get. Make sure the pack is made of durable material such as rip-stop nylon, *Gortex,* or canvas. The daypack is referred to as your "24." This pack should contain the food and gear to sustain you in the field for at least twenty-four hours.

Next, find a backpack (internal or external frame) in which you can stow the daypack plus additional gear. A backpack will cost between $50-$400 depending on the quality. Make sure this pack has outside pockets including one in front for a map. This pack will be used to hold the extra food, supplies, clothing, foul weather gear, maps, and water as well as a toothbrush. Some searchers carry a towel, soap and washcloth, toothbrush and paste, and several extra pair of socks and underwear. A backpack is referred to as your "48–hour" pack.

You must be able to survive at least forty-eight hours with no assistance, using only what you carry in this pack. I also carry extra gloves, extra scent article bags (*Ziploc* type) and extra dog food. This pack will remain in your vehicle at base camp to use when you come in from the field. Make sure the pack and straps are comfortable and fit you well.

The daypack will be on your back on search and rescue operations. I also carry a fanny pack, and in urban and criminal searches I carry only the fanny pack, in which I carry both my advanced first aid kit and my canine first aid kit.

Once you have loaded everything into the pack, try it on. It will probably weigh more than you think! Dump everything out and prioritize, getting rid of the extra stuff that you would be most likely to pitch out first in the field. Your daypack may weigh twenty pounds and your backpack may weigh eighty pounds. Whatever the weight, remember that you are the one that will have to carry it for many hours and many miles in the field.

Some other things that are very handy to have include gaiters (nylon leggings to keep lower legs dry), a radio harness to carry your radio, a headlamp (with extra batteries), ball cap to keep the sun out of your eyes, and for the experienced rescuer, a seat harness and rappel harness for the dog.

As you gain experience in different types of searches using different types of skills in different terrain you will find that you will add and delete items from your pack. One of the most important investments you can make is in a good compass. I recommend the *Silva Ranger,* made by the Silva company. It is a durable and easy-to-use field instrument. Always carry a good compass, a small notebook, memo pad, and pencil.

A newer tool for navigation is available now. It is called a Global Positioning System (GPS) and is a hand-held device that communicates with several navigation satellites. It gives you your fixed location, some devices map your movements and it helps to navigate through rough terrain. It is often used in pinpointing locations for pickup of injured persons as well. A hand-held GPS unit will cost between $150-$500. It does take some time to learn to use this tool, but it is an excellent addition to your pack.

Equipment should be stored in a "response ready" fashion. Make sure that the dog's duffel bag and your gear are together in an accessible area. Many searchers have been awakened in the middle of the night and have wasted valuable time gathering equipment together before responding. The delay may result in the team being left behind.

Appropriate clothing can make a big difference in the field. First, you must have excellent footgear. A sturdy pair of boots which fit comfortably and have a lug sole for traction are a must in the field. Boots which extend up and over the ankle are best for searching. I tried several kinds of boots, including mountain climbing boots (which were much too stiff), before I settled on a relatively new product made of leather with *Gortex* uppers and a lug sole. The boots are lightweight (less than one pound each), wear very well and keep my feet warm and dry, even through creeks. Boots will vary in cost, but remember that you get what you pay for. *Never* wear tennis shoes or any other kind of recreational shoe in the field.

Next, you will need some good outerwear. This includes a winter parka or coat and a summer jacket. Both should be brightly colored and fit easily over the clothes you will wear in the field. Most handlers overdress for the field; dress in layers so that you can remove one layer of clothing at a time to maintain a comfortable body temperature, without risking either hypothermia (a dangerous lowering of the body core temperature) or hyperthermia (a rise in body core temperature). *Gortex, Thinsulate*, rip-stop nylon and wool are excellent outerwear cloth. You will need to invest in a good pair of long underwear. Polypropylene is a cloth which provides warmth without overheating, allows perspiration to be wicked away and off the body and costs between $25-$50. Choose the style or material you feel comfortable with, remembering that once cotton is wet it stays wet. Polypropylene and wool will keep you drier and warmer even if you do get wet.

Good working gloves are a must regardless of whether the dog is worked on- or off-lead. For those people working a dog on-lead it is crucial that you get gloves that protect your hands from the lead and the elements. Weightlifter's gloves that have no fingertips, allow free movement and protect the hand are a good choice. I sewed a thick piece of leather to the palm area of my gloves for added protection. Gloves need to provide warmth as well as protection. Some handlers opt to wear polypropylene glove inserts under the lifter's gloves for additional warmth. The key is finding gloves that keep the hands warm while allowing for full movement of the hands to work the dog.

I always keep dry, comfortable clothing and tennis shoes in the car for the long ride home. This is especially important if you have gotten wet or dirty in the field while searching.

Unacceptable clothing includes tennis shoes, shorts, attire which carries derogatory slogans or pictures, and in some areas includes wearing blue jeans. Some areas require that you appear in the field wearing wool clothing only. Find out what your local regulations are and dress accordingly. Although search missions are not a fashion show, they are also not a place to wear inappropriate or inadequate clothing.

Your basic personal equipment will cost between $300-$500 depending on the brand and quality you choose. Working equipment for your dog will range in cost from $100-$250. The lifespan of this equipment depends on three main factors: first, it depends on the quality of the equipment you purchased; second, on how you take care of the equipment; and third, on the activity and types of use to which the equipment is subjected. When making your purchases, be sure that what you are buying is something to which you willingly entrust your life.

TRANSPORTATION TO A MISSION

Each rescuer should evaluate their transportation needs. Many rescuers invest thousands of dollars in up-to-date four-wheel-drive vehicles. Although most searches occur in rural areas or backcountry areas, it is feasible to respond to a search in a two-wheel–drive vehicle. The off-road capability of the four-wheel–drive is necessary if you will be searching in the backcountry or in rugged terrain.

I recommend that a barrier device be placed in a vehicle to prevent the dog from being pitched forward into the driver in the event of a sudden stop or accident. Some handlers choose to transport dogs in a crate. Either way, the dogs must be protected from injury or from interfering with the driver in the event of a sudden stop or an accident. The barrier will also prevent the dog from dislodging the gear shift which could cause the vehicle to roll or engage. It is better to insist that the dog remain behind the barrier than to risk an accident.

Make sure your vehicle is serviced regularly and always keep good tires on your vehicle. If you live in an area with severe winters, be sure that you have winter tires, chains, or other traction devices. Be prepared to respond in the crummiest weather at the worst possible times!

When traveling by air, it may become necessary to transport the dog in a crate. Crates are made by a number of manufacturers and range in cost from $60-$150. Be sure that the crate you purchase will accommodate your dog when it is full grown. The dog must be able to sit, stand up and turn around easily. I currently use a crate manufactured from molded plastic. The top and bottom separate for cleaning and are held together by twelve locking screws. The empty crates are light enough to be picked up by one person yet are sturdy enough for transportation through an airport baggage system.

Most crate manufacturers sell a grate for the bottom of the crate, but it is seldom sold with the crate so be sure to ask for one. The grate allows air to circulate beneath the dog and will minimize the mess should the dog foul the crate while in transit. The grate sells for about $20-$40 and is a worthwhile investment. I also throw a blanket, sheepskin pad or towel in for the dog to lie on and I toss in a chew toy.

Once you have your crate be sure to mark it. Using waterproof paint or markers, stencil your name and phone number clearly on the top of the crate in large letters. Also stencil "Search Dog" or "Search and Rescue Dog" clearly on both sides of the crate. Be sure that you attach an airline label with your name, address and phone number clearly marked.

For added security I attach a cable-type bicycle lock with a combination padlock. I thread the cable through the side vents and lock it using the crate door as an anchor. This prevents the door of the crate from popping open while in transit and prevents someone from letting the dog out of the crate. The locks sell for about $6. Another security item is to buy some plastic, six-inch wire ties at a hardware store. Run one wire tie through each screw hole in the side of the crate and tighten it by passing the tongue through the locking device on the wire tie. Cut the extra wire tie end off. Then press the crate screw through the hole and attach the nut. This will add an extra locking device to make sure that, should the screw fall out, the crate will remain together.

A few of the major airlines will allow a search dog to ride in the passenger cabin of the aircraft. The airlines require that the dog be controlled at all times, be friendly, and be attended by the handler at all times. There may or may not be a charge for this service. Other airlines require that the dog be shipped in the baggage compartment but will transport the dog for free. There are still other airlines that do not recognize search dogs and require that the dog be shipped in the baggage compartment, charging a standard fee for the shipping.

If you are allowed to transport the dog in the passenger cabin, be sure to bring a crate along, as baggage, in the event that the dog does not travel well in the cabin, or is dirty from searching and needs to be crated on the way home. I prefer to crate the dogs if possible, as there are always a few people on the plane that are allergic to dogs or that complain, and I prefer to concentrate on what lies ahead or to rest up after a search.

If you are shipping the dog to someone else, be sure that the person's name, address and phone number are attached to the crate. I also label the crate with "Heavy! Use at least 2 people to lift!" Ben weighs well over a hundred and ten pounds and I want baggage handlers to know before they try to lift him. Several search and show dogs have suffered permanent injuries from being dropped in crates.

Don't invest in every piece of equipment at once. Make sure that search and rescue is something you are committed to before you invest the money. Spread your costs over time by buying only that which is relevant and useful at your skill level.

SUGGESTED EQUIMENT KITS
THAT ARE EASY TO ASSEMBLE

DAYPACK

Batteries
  (2 extra sets for headlamp and flashlight)
Compass
Human first aid kit
Flashlight (plastic)
50' of 500-lb. test line
Insect repellent
Map of search area
Notebook
Pencils (2)
Radio batteries (1-2)
Headlamp (lightweight, lithium)
6" ruler marked in 10ths of inches
Signal mirror (small hand-held type)
Stocking cap (wool)
Survival kit (pre-packaged)
Whistle
12 Gloves (disposable rubber exam type)

Flashlight bulb (2 extra)
Headlamp bulb (2 extra)
Fire starter
Canine first aid kit
Food (4 "no cook" meals)
Gloves (2 pair—wool and leather)
Knife (folding type or pocket knife)
Matches (36 waterproofed in
  plastic container)
Radio (2-way hand-held)
2" candle stub
Flares (2-4)
Shelter (9' x 12' tarp)
Snacks (high-energy type)
Sun block (cream or lotion)
Water bottle (1 qt.)
Webbing (50' of 1" heavyweight)

MISSION PACK (48 hours or longer)

Batteries (3 sets)
Boots (lug or *Vibram* sole)
Fire starter (commercial)
Food (4 meals that require cooking)
Hygiene items (toothbrush, soap, etc.)
Matches (60 waterproofed)
Pants (1 pair wool, 1 pair sweats)
Pencils (2)
Purification tabs (36)
Rain pants (loose fitting)
Shirts (1-2 wool shirts)
Sleeping bag (*Hollofil* or down)
Sleeping pad (*Ensolite* or mattress)
Socks (2 pair wool, 2 pair cotton)
Stove fuel (1 bottle)
Water bottles (2 one-quart size)

Drink Mixes (both hot and cold)
Candy (hard candy)
Flares (4 day or night type)
Gloves (wool and rubber)
Map of area being searched
Mess kit & and eating utensils
Notebook (small)
Protractor (360-degree type)
Raincoat (poncho/jacket with hood)
Ruler
Signal mirror (small hand-held)
Sleeping bag cover (waterproof)
Snacks ("no cook" high energy)
Stove (lightweight, easy operation)
Tent (2-person)
Whistle

SUGGESTED EQUIMENT KITS
THAT ARE EASY TO ASSEMBLE
(continued)

SURVIVAL KIT

Band-Aids (12 of assorted sizes)
Bouillon cubes (12)
Candy (1 lb. hard type)
Disposable cups (2)
Matches (36 waterproofed)
Mirror (small hand-held)
Needle (2 large)
Pencil (2)
Safety pins (6 extra large)
Soup mix (6 packets of instant)
Thread (1 large spool of size 10)
Whistle
Aspirin (24)
Sewing kit w/needle (small)
12 fishing hooks

Beverages (6 packets of instant)
Candle (4" plumber's candle)
Cord (20' of nylon parachute type)
Emery paper (sandpaper 4" x 4")
Metal cup (1 large for heating water)
Moleskin (6" x 6" sheet)
Notebook
Razor blade (single-edged, taped)
Shelter (2 extra-large trash bags)
Tea Bags (12)
Tube tent (2-person)
Sugar packets (24)
Insect repellent
Pocketknife (small)
100' 10-lb. test fishing line

HUMAN FIRST AID KIT

Acetaminophen (24 tablets)
Alcohol pads (12 individually wrapped)
Antihistamine tabs (24 tablets)
Band-Aids (24 of assorted sizes)
Cup (1)
Emergency blanket
Gauze (2 rolls of 2")
Ibuprofen (24 tablets)
Needle (2 large)
Pencil (2)
Rubber gloves (2 pair disposable)
Triangular bandage (2)
Tweezers (1)

Adhesive tape (1 roll of 2")
Antibacterial (Neosporin or similar)
Aspirin (24 tablets)
Compress bandages (4)
Elastic bandage (2-2", 1-3", 1-4")
Eyewash (1 bottle *Artificial Tears*)
Gauze pads (10 pads 4" x 4")
Moleskin (6" x 6" sheet)
Paper (small tablet)
Purification tabs (36)
Salt tablets (1 small bottle)
Tube tent (2-person size)
Chapstick (1 tube)

SUGGESTED EQUIMENT KITS
THAT ARE EASY TO ASSEMBLE
(continued)

CANINE FIRST AID KIT

Alcohol pads (24 individually wrapped)
Antibacterial (Neosporin or Panalog)
Anti-diarrhea (12 tablets)
Band-Aids (12 large fabric style)
Electrolyte powder (1 pkg. instant)
Epinephrine
Gauze pads (12 sterile 4", 12-2" x 2")
IV catheters (as applicable)
Moleskin (2 sheets 6" x 6")
Nitrofurazone (3 dressings of 2%)
Safety pins (6 extra large)
Stomach tube (from veterinarian)
Stretch adhesive (2 rolls of 4")
Suture kit
Tape (2 rolls of 2" *Zonas* brand)
Tweezers (1)

Antacids (24 chewable type)
Antibiotics (12 tablets)
Aspirin tablets (12)
Cotton balls (24)
Emergency drugs
Eyewash (1 plastic 4-ounce bottle)
Ice pack (Instant chemical type)
Lactated Ringer's (1 liter bag)
Nail clippers (1 pair large)
Ophthalmic ointment (1 tube)
Snake bite kit (1 pre-packaged)
Styptic powder (1 small container)
Stretch gauze (2 4" Kling type)
Swabs (36 cotton-tip applicators)
Triangular bandage (4)

BASIC DOG CARE EQUIPMENT

Brush (coat conditioning)
Ear cleaner (solution, pads or similar)
Eyewash
First aid kit (canine type)
Food (high-quality dry variety)
Shedding blade
Toothbrush
Toothpaste
Vitamins (as specified by breeder or
    veterinarian)

Crate (transportation/shelter)
Kennel or fenced yard (8'x10')
Dish (1 stainless steel 4-5 qt. size)
Rubber exam gloves—disposable
Nail clippers
Shelter (doghouse or similar
    indoor shelter)
Toys (tennis balls, etc.)
Water bucket (10-quart rubber or
    stainless steel)

**SUGGESTED EQUIMENT KITS
THAT ARE EASY TO ASSEMBLE
(continued)**

TRAINING EQUIPMENT

Blanket
Collar—working
Harness
10-ft. lead—fieldwork
18-in. lead—traffic

Collar—basic
Gloves
4-ft. lead—criminal
6-ft. lead—standard
Treats

FIELD WORKING EQUIPMENT

Can opener (P-38 military type)
Collar (nylon web)
Stainless steel dish (4 qt.)
Electrolyte powder (1 pkg. instant)
Gear bag
Harness
10-ft. lead—fieldwork
18-in. lead—traffic
Water bottles

Canned food
Collar (chain type)
Dry food packed in plastic bags
First aid kit
Gloves (2 pair)
4-ft. lead—criminal
6-ft. lead—standard
Scent article kit
Water bucket

HANDLER TRAINING

Handlers as well as dogs need constant training to learn and to maintain search skills; training begins with foundation basics like human and canine first aid and CPR.

Map and compass training is crucial for every handler. A handler must be able to read a variety of maps including survey maps, Forest Service maps, aeronautical maps and gridded search maps. Training should include the use of township, range and section in determining a location and the use of longitude and latitude to find a specific point and handlers should also be able to find their field location from base camp.

Compass training is essential for any field worker as the ability to pinpoint your location using a compass and map may be crucial when you locate a victim. Compass courses are available through many different sources. Ground search units, such as Explorer Search and Rescue, offer excellent courses in map and compass training.

If you cannot find anyone to teach you to use a map and compass, contact your local Boy or Girl Scouts of America office. The Explorer Scouts as well as the Boy and Girl Scouts teach map and compass courses regularly. You might also contact an orienteering or hiking club. Check with the local Parks Department, or State or National Parks office for additional resources.

Familiarity with a portable radio and radio communications is very important because radios are the primary means of communication during any search operation. Handlers must be familiar with the portable radio they carry, how to operate it, how to make minor field repairs and battery changes.

Intermediate training includes night searches and advanced courses in human and canine first aid. Some options for advanced training include search management and water, disaster and criminal pursuit training. Courses in managing disaster scenes, urban rescue, the use of heavy equipment, tunnel rescue, disaster forensics, the role of support teams and related topics are also popular now. Dealing with disaster victims, risks and risk management for volunteers, critical incident stress and debriefing, rescues involving hydraulics and low angle dams, high angle and mountain rescues, managing large search operations, dealing with politically sensitive searches and other high profile situations are often presented at workshops and seminars.

It is recommended that handlers successfully complete at least forty hours of classroom training each year in addition to regular field training. It is your responsibility to make sure that your field skills are sharp. In reality, forty hours of training is very little time.

HANDLER TRAINING RECORDS

It is critical that you keep written records of the types of training you have taken. Seminars, conferences, classroom or field training must be documented just as you should document the work of the dog. Documenting your training provides proof of your willingness to prepare and work toward a high level of skills for the dog team. As in any profession, documentation reflects experience to potential clients and other potential team members.

The training record format can be as simple or as complex as you want. If you belong to an organized search team the group will often have a training record form. It should contain basic information about you (full name, address and phone number, date of birth, medical problems, allergies, blood type and emergency contact person), and there should be a section on the form for basic skills to be listed such as human first aid and CPR, as well as canine first aid and CPR. The expiration date for these certifications should be noted so that arrangements can be made to re-certify.

The form should also have a series of blanks to record any courses taken in wilderness survival, map and compass and basic search training. The remainder of the form should have room to list advanced training like emergency management, night navigation, winter survival, helicopter familiarization, as well as any conferences and seminars you may have attended.

The record should be updated at least once a year but it is much simpler to update your records following each training event that you attend. Your training record folder should also include copies of any certificates or awards you have received.

SEMINARS AND CONFERENCES

Several search and rescue organizations hold seminars or specialized training forums on an annual basis and several individual states hold annual Search and Rescue Conferences. The National Association for Search and Rescue has annual conferences, as does The National Police Bloodhound Association, National K-9 Rescue and several other organizations. All of these seminars include a lecture and many include field work on both beginning and advanced levels. Training may be for the handler only, others include the dogs.

Some seminars and training conferences are expensive to attend. There may be a tuition fee as well as costs for transportation, lodging, and food. Some organizations may offer handlers reduced rates or scholarships to help defray the costs and some civic groups may donate money to help pay for a training session.

Find out the specifics of any training session before you make arrangements to go. Training conferences may focus on a specific type of rescue resource, such as disaster dogs, and may not be relevant to all handlers. Remember, there are many different interests in the working dog community. In the wake of several recent disasters, disaster rescue has received a lot of attention. There are a number of conferences and seminars that deal with this kind of search problem only. Following earthquakes in Mexico City, Armenia and San Franciso, the bombing in Oklahoma and several building collapses, the SAR community has renewed focus on this kind of training. A number of experienced teams have come forward to conduct training.

Before attending find out if you have the basic criteria for attendance. For example, if your dog is a wilderness search dog but you have no intention of working disasters, pass up this kind of training. Many seminars focus on advanced level dog teams. It doesn't hurt to attend the training but leave your dog at home. Take advantage of learning from and working with an experienced team. Advanced level training is more for you, at this point, than the dog. Specific kinds of training may vary. Wilderness search training often includes handler clinics. Clinics in map and compass, land navigation, helicopter safety, survival, lost person behavior, teamwork and search management are popular. There may be sessions on scent, scent articles and how weather and terrain affect a search dog's working methods. Obstacle training and practical field work for teams may also be available.

The primary focus of water search seminars is drownings, floodings and disaster work. There may be training in a practical field problem involving the use of scuba divers or a cadaver scent machine. Some water search seminars provide the handler with classroom instruction only, while others include a balanced portion of field as well as classroom work. Seminars also provide opportunities for networking and training materials. One of the premier researchers and trainers for water search work is Marian Hardy, who has conducted extensive reviews of water search missions and is actively involved in working and training a search dog.

Disaster seminars may offer basic and advanced levels of search techniques, handler and dog safety, basic construction and collapse theory, and rubble, water and mud searching. Field work in disaster training often includes working in partially demolished buildings, rubble piles and heaps of debris.

Crime scene and criminal work seminars are hard to find. This training usually includes drug work, pursuit, evidence and crime scene work and scent and scent articles. Basic crime scene investigation, working with investigators, courtroom testimony, preparing reports, working with police canines, and scent discrimination are detailed for new handlers. Law enforcement related topics are the focus of this training. These seminars are often closed to civilians but it is possible, with some effort, to set up the same kind of training on your own.

Some seminars are closed to the novice handler or limited to member attendance only. It is becoming increasingly difficult to find classes geared for the new handler at many national seminars. Many handlers feel that there is far too much swapping of "war stories" than actual training at many seminars. Check with the seminar sponsor to find out if the training they are offering is something you can use. Find out if there will be any field work or mock searches allowing the dogs to work. If the seminar is classroom only or targeted at a more advanced level than your team, leave your dog at home. The added expense and time is wasted if your dog cannot work.

Many conferences are a forum for individuals to present papers, slides, or research on specific topics. They usually have a question-and-answer period for participants to find out more information. Unfortunately, there are very few open forums in which handlers can exchange ideas, successes, failures and training tips.

A newcomer to the field may feel pushed aside at conferences. Handlers recall successes and advancements that the new handler may not understand. Be aware that experienced handlers will probably not walk up and introduce themselves. At a national conference I attended I listened to various experts talk about searches, methods and responses. I watched as new handlers' questions and ideas were ignored or skeptically listened to. It is a tough experience for the new handlers. They were excited to learn from the experiences of the seasoned veterans.

There is a lot of competition between groups providing the same kind of resource. The competition shouldn't be there. It seems that the purpose, to save lives, is often lost in the politics. Groups grow and change with time and experience. Often the goal is lost in the chaos of leadership and politics. Experienced handlers have much to offer. It is always nice when a veteran handler offers to assist the novice and working with them can often be the best method of training. Novices often bring a fresh perspective to training that veteran handlers can use and develop. Each handler works a little differently and there may be a number of ways to do the same thing, none of which are wrong. No one person has all of the answers.

Check with search and rescue organizations to find out training calendars and look for the conference or seminar that best fits your needs and desires for training. Attendance at one or two outside training seminars a year will be plenty for most handlers.

BASIC OBEDIENCE

Basic obedience training is essential for every dog. A badly behaved dog is a liability on searches and a detriment to society. A domestic dog, like a wild dog, wants to be accepted by its pack—and *you* are its pack. Good behavior is a mandatory prerequisite to human acceptance and, therefore, it is the handler's responsibility to the dog to provide the necessary training.

Basic obedience tasks include coming when called, stopping when told, sitting and lying down on command. These basic commands are ones that will be necessary in the field, during transportation and when taking the dog out in public. This training will lay the foundation that is so crucial in the field and it is therefore necessary that the person who will be handling the dog is also the person who is training it. The dog learns to read the handler much like the handler reads the dog.

Equipment used in training includes a training collar (also called a "choke chain"), a six-foot lead, a fifteen- to twenty-foot lead and treats for the dog. Liver or cheese is almost every dog's favorite treat and plenty of treats should be at hand for rewarding the dog's performance. A tennis ball or other favorite toy should be used during playtime following the training session.

Success in obedience training is based on rewarding good behavior and correcting mistakes. Through clear verbal displeasure and quick correction the dog will learn the difference between a major error and something that can be reversed quickly. Keep in mind that perfection is something achieved only after lots of hard work.

When the dog performs incorrectly the handler must *immediately* express displeasure, by saying "No!" in a clear, firm voice. The handler should then correct the action of the dog. After the correction repeat the command to allow the dog to complete the direction correctly. Corrections must be firm enough to gain the dog's attention without becoming a physical power conflict or becoming overly harsh. Praise should follow all actions that are done correctly whether done right the first time or done right after a correction. Be generous with your praise. Make sure that praise is accompanied by physical attention such as a pat and a quick scratch behind the ears.

Remember, harsh discipline such as physically or verbally assaulting a dog will only reinforce the negative behavior. A training period must be something the dog looks forward to, not something the dog will resent or resist out of fear of verbal battery or physical pain. Think about what makes you want to learn. Do you eagerly await a lesson that ends in reward or one that ends in pain and embarrassment?

Success is something we should always work towards in basic training. Obedience training makes the dog more socially successful. Some Bloodhounds excel at obedience, and a well-trained Bloodhound going through the obedience paces is phenomenal to watch.

While many handlers use food rewards for training and during missions, I only use food rewards in the very beginning of training. I encourage the dog to find the person, not the treat, because in the field the dog must want to find the missing person to receive the praise, not a food reward.

Schedule training at a regular time every day. Training periods need not be more than fifteen minutes long and should never exceed thirty minutes in the first stages of training. Remember that long training periods become opportunities for distractions, frustration and boredom. Keep the sessions focused on one task until the dog performs the task promptly and consistently and then move on to another task.

Individual dogs will learn at different paces. Some dogs will quickly master basic obedience while others will struggle with each new task. Gear your training periods according to your dog's learning style. By providing a short play period *after* the training session, the dog will work eagerly through training to get to the play period. Don't start a training period with playtime because the dog will not understand the sudden shift from playing and roughhousing to serious and demanding instructions.

Some handlers become easily frustrated when their dog does not perform simple or complex tasks on the first request. Handlers who are easily frustrated and lose their temper will lose control of their dog. You must control the training sessions; don't allow the dog to control you. Discipline is apt to be overly harsh when the handler has become frustrated and is trying to regain control of the training session. Be firm and fair, but above all, be consistent with the dog.

Work the dog in a variety of locations to get him used to obeying you regardless of where you might be. Busy streets, parks, school grounds, crowds, and open country should not affect how your dog performs once he has learned the basic tasks.

BASIC COMMANDS

Basic obedience commands for all working dogs include "Sit," "Down," "Come" and "Kennel." The "Sit," "Down" and "Come" commands will aid you in the field. The "Kennel" command will aid you in loading your dogs in a vehicle and putting them in a crate for shipping, securing, or sleeping. Other commands which are important include "Up," "Easy," "Find" and "Out." To avoid confusion I have defined each term as follows:

"Sit!"	the dog should sit upright when instructed.
"Down!"	the dog lies down immediately.
"Come!"	the dog comes directly to the handler.
"Kennel!"	the dog goes directly where indicated.
"Up!"	teaches the dog to look up or climb up.
"Easy!"	teaches the dog to slow down.
"Find!"	the start command on the trail.
"Out!"	the dog should stop what he is doing.
"OK!"	release command allows the dog to relax.

The first lesson for any dog is to come when the handler calls. Start with your dog on a six-foot lead and begin walking. Change direction quickly and with a quick, sharp tug call the dog to you saying, "Digger, come!" and stop. If the dog does not immediately come, give the lead a firm pull and repeat the command. Praise the dog for doing it right. Repeat the instruction until the dog responds immediately. Don't stand and jerk the dog back and forth. Move away, call the dog and tug the lead. You may want to use a treat for this beginning lesson.

Another way to accomplish this is to begin walking, pause, then call the dog, running backwards away from him. As the dog runs toward you, stop and allow the dog to come up to you, praising him for a job well done. Make the lessons quick and fun. Practice until the dog comes when called.

Move the training to a place where there are some distractions and repeat the lessons so that the dog will come when called regardless of distractions or location. I practice in the park, strip malls, parking lots and walking down the street. Remember that there may be times the dog is distracted so try to work patiently through them.

To teach a dog to sit, call the dog to you and align him with your left side. Give him the command, "Digger, sit!" and pull the lead straight up while pushing down on his rear. The lead should be in your right hand so that your left hand can push down to get him in the right position. Praise him for sitting and then step forward and give him the release command. Praise the dog again and repeat the exercise. Once he masters this, start adding distractions.

Practice the "Sit!" command before you walk through a doorway. Have the dog wait until you have cleared the doorway and then call him. Move the exercise outside and practice on walks, in the car, and when you are out training in the field. This command teaches the dog to wait until you are ready for him to move. You can practice the "Sit!" command by having dog sit before you put the dinner pan down or before opening a door.

Once the dog has learned to "Come!" and to "Sit!" it is time to move on to the second level of commands. Remember to be consistent and go slowly to ensure that the dog is successful at one thing before starting something new. Do not overburden the dog at a training session but review the previous session and begin a new command only when the dog demonstrates clear understanding of the previous lessons.

CRATE TRAINING

My hounds travel in crates for their safety. I do not believe in transporting working dogs untethered in an open truck; I believe that the dog is valuable and deserves safety during transportation. Some of my hounds have also slept in crates or kennels. You will probably have to teach a dog to go into a kennel or crate since they would much rather make their own decisions where they will sleep, spend time or travel.

I start all of my puppies sleeping in crates so that they know that they have one place in the house that is theirs. I start by taking the door off the crate and setting it aside. I find a treat the puppy loves and toss it just inside the doorway so that the puppy can lean in and grab it. The next toss requires that the puppy lean in much further or even step into the doorway to get the treat. Eventually the pup has to go all the way in and fetch the treat from the very back of the crate. Success is declared when the pup will trot in immediately and pick up the treat.

Next I put the door back on and repeat the process. Hold the puppy's collar, toss the treat, give the "Kennel!" command and let go. Once the puppy goes right in, I close the door after him, giving him a small treat and lots of praise before letting him out. Each time I wait a few seconds longer before release, then a few minutes. Eventually you leave the room for a minute, five minutes and so on. This gradually reinforces that they have not been abandoned.

I repeat the exercise in any situation I will be using the "Kennel!" command, such as loading into the car, into a crate in the van or going into a kennel at bedtime. I also use the command when putting the dogs into the play yard and kennel outside. The command indicates that the dog should enter any area, crate or place that you request.

Once the puppy has accomplished this it is time to leash him and practice approaching the crate in other new or unique situations—perhaps in a different location or kenneling the dog without a treat. Have the dog on-lead and walk up to the open doorway of the crate. Put your hand on the dog's collar and push forward at the same time saying "Kennel!"

It is important to realize that some dogs may experience claustrophobia in a crate. Until they realize that they are not going to be confined to the crate indefinitely and that the crate is not going to hurt them they may refuse or struggle or behave badly. For claustrophobic dogs or dogs reluctant to enter a crate there a few things you can do to build their confidence and crate train them as well. Try breaking the crate down and walking the dog into the bottom half, allowing him to see all around him. Walk him right back out. You can feed a dog in a crate or part of a crate to encourage familiarity. Every time you walk the dog into the partial crate give the "Kennel!" command. As he becomes more confident gradually reconstruct the crate, repeating the exercises and feeding him at each stage. Finally add the door and increase the amount of time spent in the crate as he is successful.

For those dogs that are afraid of crates, try to find the reason behind this. It may be simply that the dog has never seen a crate before or it may be because he was abused in a crate or was transported in a crate that was dropped or rolled or was exposed to a similar frightening experience. It will take time to get the dog used to a crate, but be firm, fair and consistent.

Remember that a puppy will whimper, whine, cry, scream and scratch at a crate from loneliness, boredom and separation from his littermates his first nights in his new home. This behavior doesn't mean he has crate phobias! It means he wants companionship and attention. Start your puppy out in a crate and in the long run, you'll be happier when he eagerly beds down in his space, loads into his kennel for shipping and seeks out his kennel for rest.

Using the same "Kennel!" command, you can teach the dog to load into a vehicle. Take the dog to the tailgate or doorway of the vehicle and, pushing forward on the collar, give the command to "Kennel!" Some handlers choose to use a "Load up!" command for vehicles, but that is up to the individual handler. Since my Bloodhounds travel in the car so often they believe it is their kennel away from home. Using "Kennel!" was much easier for them to understand. Praise the dog for correctly loading up on command.

"EASY!"

One of the most important things you can do for yourself is to teach a dog not to drag you. It is not only beneficial to you on a long trail, it also allows you to control the dog more effectively. In the field you need to be able to control the dog to prevent him from dragging you into danger, off embankments, into holes or off cliffs.

With the dog on a six-foot lead, start walking and allow the dog to get to the end of the lead. Pull back firmly and at the same time say "Easy!" simultaneously releasing the pressure on the lead. Praise the dog for allowing slack in the lead and repeat the command. Practice this again and again.

Once the dog immediately slows down and stops pulling on command, move your training to the park, mall, in town or in other areas with lots of distractions. Work on this until the dog has mastered it. Allowing a dog to drag you on a lead is not only physically exhausting, it also increases the chances of the dog speeding up and missing evidence or a turn in the trail, and increases your chances of falling.

Make sure that you work and walk your dog at a pace you can maintain. Running behind the dog will quickly lead to exhaustion. In urgent cases you or the dog may miss an important turn or not see a sudden drop-off, and you may fall or be injured. You must remain in control.

"OUT!"

The "Out!" command is used to stop the dog from whatever he is doing, be it accepting food, eating garbage, or harassing another dog. When you use the "Out!" command the dog knows to stop immediately. When working a trail, the dog is following his nose, not his common sense. A porcupine, a skunk or a snake can quickly end your trail and could cause permanent damage. The dog must be taught to stop on command.

The "Out!" command is taught by allowing the dog to become interested in something other than you. Take him for a walk on a short lead and as he sniffs the shrubbery, abruptly and firmly tug back on the lead saying "Out!" in a firm voice. Break the dog's attention to the object, then praise him. If he just goes back to the same thing repeat the strong tug and the "Out!" command. When he does not go back to the object, praise him. Pull him up close to you to make sure that he understands he is to stay away. Practice this, increasing the lead length and reinforcing the lesson.

Pull the dog back quickly and without hesitation. Reward the dog for stopping and repeat the exercise. If the dog stops to sniff at a pile of feces or lunges at someone or something either in excitement or anger, use the "Out!" command clearly and stop the dog from continuing. I use the "Out!" command to steer the dogs away from the table, the cat box, groceries in the car, even people.

I also use the "Out!" command on the trail when the dog stops to mark his territory at the base camp before we begin a trail. Dogs urinating all over a base camp is ridiculous. My dogs learned that other than marking the beginning of their trails, they are not allowed to stop to sniff around for other dogs or mark their territory. I want their total attention on the missing person, not on satisfying their natural urge to leave their mark.

Another good reason to teach a dog the "Out!" command is in the event that he gets into something that is poisonous or that he shouldn't be eating. No one should feed your dogs *anything* that you haven't approved of.

It is better to be safe and forbid anyone to feed your dogs without your permission than to have a dog get sick or even die from the wrong thing. Many dogs have the "eat first and question later" mentality. Many well-meaning people will feed the dog out of thinking it is just a treat; they don't understand that working dogs are on a carefully balanced diet of quality food and supplements designed to keep them in top shape. The diet is designed to provide nutrition and calories for the field. Sugar and junk food are no better for dogs than they are for the handlers!

Another instance in which the "Out!" command is useful is when the trail suddenly disappears over a cliff or you have to end a trail. Or you may stumble, twist an ankle, fall or just need to take a break. Use the "Out!" command to stop the dog. Some dogs will not want to leave a deceased body alone and it will be necessary to issue the "Out!" command to get them to move away. Practice using the "Out!" command in a variety of situations and locations until the dog stops what he is doing and waits for your next direction.

"UP!"

The "Up!" command is used to get the dog to look above him or to climb up. Running trails where the runner is above the dog will encourage the dog to respond to "Up!" It also helps teach the dog to get his head up and use the wind or vegetation to pick up scent.

I start puppies on the "Up!" command at mealtime. I have their feed pan in my hand and say "Up!" When they look up I praise them and put their dish down. Simple. I allow my dogs to rise up on their hind legs, putting their paws on my chest or shoulders only with permission. This also reinforces the "Up!" command.

Some trails may end with the victim in a tree and the dog must be able to look up to follow the scent. Ben and I were looking for a missing adolescent who was involved in playing a game called "Dungeons and Dragons" when he disappeared. After hasty teams failed to locate the boy we were called out. It was getting dark and visibility was poor as the trail led from a park into a wooded area. Ben worked into the woods and began air scenting and whining. He stopped and looked off to one side of the trail. Taking a bearing right off the end of his nose we worked into a brushy stand of trees. Ben jumped up and looked up the tree. When I looked up my headlamp illuminated the dead boy's body hanging in the tree.

In another case we chased an assault suspect through a residential area and into the woods. The suspect crossed a creek, ran down the other side and then climbed a tree. Ben, working the air, crossed the creek right under the tree and jumped up on the trunk. The suspect, knowing he was cornered, screamed, "Call him off! I'll come down! Don't let him get me!" Ben stood waiting and wagging his tail as the suspect climbed down and was led away in handcuffs. I forgot to tell the suspect that Ben didn't bite.

To teach the dog the command in the field, try having someone climb a short distance up either a tree or on stable playground equipment. We use the slide at the playground. The dog can see the ladder and follow it, visually and physically, up. Have the person wave and call the dog to get him to look up at the same time you give the "Up!" command. As the dog begins to look up on command have your runner move out of sight from the dog, climbing a tree or up on a roof or on a fence.

To teach the dog to look up at trees have your runner climb a short distance up the tree. Take the dog to the tree and, while saying "Up!" slap the tree in an upward motion towards

The handler is the "alpha" in a team.
ILLUSTRATION BY
CRYSTAL MELVIN

the person. Have the person call the dog saying "Up! Up!" Using a treat to teach the dog is also a simple method. Hold the treat up against the object and command the dog "Up!" to reach the treat, praising him for correct action.

The "Up" command can also be used when loading the dog into a transport vehicle. Remember to practice the command in training to duplicate potential scenarios in the field.

When you are training your dog remember to give the command *once* and allow the dog to perform the task. Nagging and repeating the command over and over will only confuse the dog. Allow the dog to perform the task and be as quick with praise as you are with correction.

My hounds are schooled in manners from day one and I find that I worry more about *people* with poor manners than I do the hounds! I know that the dogs will lie at my feet during a lecture and stand quietly for pats and pets later. I also know that when I tell them to lie down or to stand still, they will. Confidence is built through practice and teamwork and it is your responsibility to train the dog; don't let the dog train you!

CHAPTER FOUR

The Paper Trail

RECORDS AND DOCUMENTATION

There is an old saying that "nothing is complete until the paperwork is done." In the world of dog training those eight words are a commandment. A handler that neglects paperwork following training and missions will lack credibility. A criminal case may not go to court for years after an incident and trying to remember exact details years after a mission is impossible without comprehensive notes. The team can easily be discredited in court and will probably never be used by police agencies.

Some agencies will refuse to work with dog teams that do not keep detailed written records. Paperwork is essential for several reasons. First, it provides a history of the team. Training records show the type of training, difficulty level and frequency of practice. They detail individual achievements and failures of the team. Accurate record keeping allows the handler to monitor the areas that need work and helps set up the next series of trails. Records can show new obstacles, distances, time spans or similar new search problems. This kind of paperwork serves to show prospective agencies that the team is well trained and reliable. It also makes a useful reference manual for court testimony, statistics and for those times you just want to reminisce!

There are four basic types of reports: canine training records, handler training records, criminal search reports and general missions reports. Check with other groups or handlers to find out what different report forms exist. Choose one of those or design a form that fits your specific needs. The important thing to remember is to keep accurate and detailed records.

Once you decide on your report format, type it and make copies. When you fill them out, complete them legibly; the writing must be easily read by other people. Some handlers choose to block print or type their reports. Be sure that you sign every report before filing it.

It is impossible to know, ahead of time, whether a lost child case will turn into a criminal case. Every search has the potential to become your worst nightmare. Never assume that a missing person will always be found. The case may not be a criminal disappearance; the missing person could simply be hiding. Some lost people just don't want to be found.

I started a comprehensive record system the day that Digger ran his first trail. My records system has continued and has been updated and expanded as the team trained in new areas. The forms I developed are used by many dog teams today because of the detail included and the general simplicity of the form. If you use a report form, you will have an advantage. You will arrive at the site ready to document the information you need. If you keep training records on a computer, it is necessary to have a hard copy of each one as well as the computer copy. This gives you a computer data file and available copies when needed. The hard copies are easily stored in a series of three-ring binders.

I suggest compiling a mission briefcase. Include blank mission report forms, briefing sheets, and plain paper. Maps, pens and pencils, an altimeter, and an outdoor thermometer are also good to include. Leave the briefcase in the vehicle that you will be using on searches. Once you arrive at the base camp complete the initial information. Before you leave the base camp complete the remainder of the report and obtain any necessary signatures. Your report is done quickly.

Another useful tool is a pocket tape recorder carried on both training sessions and missions. This allows you to make verbal notes as you are working; a tape recorder is easier to carry and you can talk while the dog works.

Another reason for detailed record keeping is to constantly upgrade the training and obstacles on which you work. Read through your training records to identify problems, and structure trails to work on those areas. Reviewing past training records is also an excellent way to critique the way that you train. If all of the training records reflect a simple trail, it is time to add difficulty. Natural obstacles and new ideas should be used often.

If the unit uses a specific form for reports make sure that everyone understands what each section means. Agree on criteria for each section and define any unclear areas.

Give a copy of any report you complete to the agency that called you. Never give your original report away; instead, make a copy of the report and send it. Sometimes when the original report is lost there are problems in getting a copy accepted. If the agency requests, have your signature notarized on the copy.

Any written report, training record or other document must be the truth. It can be tempting to overstate the qualifications of your team to receive more call-outs or honors. It is not worth the embarrassment or potential criminal prosecution.

There are handlers that don't document trails that are inconclusive or missions in which the victim is found by another searcher. The handler may blame failures on a contaminated scent article, incorrect information or find some environmental or terrain problem to explain the dog's performance. They may claim that the ground was too wet (or too dry), the wind was blowing too hard (or not hard enough), the terrain was too rugged (or too open) to hold a scent, or the weather was too hot (or too cold) for trailing. Often these people will claim that they have thousands of hours of training time but no records to prove it.

Document all of your successes and failures. Remember that credibility is built through honesty. There have been a few times I chose to pull one of the dogs off the trail because it didn't seem like they were working. If the dog was working the right direction or trail, the search report for the missions or training trail will be marked "handler error" on the narrative and a written explanation of what happened will be included. Every handler will struggle with believing in the dog from time to time. Document it and try not to let it happen again.

PROOF OF REGISTRATION

For general search and rescue work it is not necessary that the working dog be purebred. There are many successful working dogs that are mixed breed. Some of these dogs are rescued from animal shelters and can be successfully trained for search and rescue or disaster work. Criminal work, however, requires purebred dogs.

The breed of the dog is less of an issue than proof of registration with a known and accepted purebred dog registry. The most common purebred dog registry in the United States is the American Kennel Club (AKC). Dogs whose parents are AKC registered are also eligible for registration with the AKC. From a historical perspective, a dog's bloodline may connect it to a line of dogs known for their abilities to work a trail. The Bloodhound in particular has a history underscoring the instinctive and genetic predisposition for trailing. The Bloodhound has been used to trail humans throughout history, and records can be produced in a court of law as evidence of reliability. A dog that can be proven to be bred from a long line of trailing hounds is even more of an asset.

If a dog is a mixed breed the historical records become less distinct. There are some cases where proof of registration is not an issue, but in general, a registered dog is accepted more readily by the legal system.

The breeder is responsible for providing the registered name and number of the sire and the dam of the litter. An AKC registration number has a one- or two-letter prefix, which indicates the breed, followed by the six numbers assigned to that particular dog. The owner of the dog is responsible for naming the dog and applying for registration. You need to fill out an application and pay a fee, following which the AKC sends the owner the appropriate registration certificate. A dog that has been registered with the AKC cannot be renamed.

Not every application submitted is granted. The name chosen may not meet the criteria established by the AKC or it may already be assigned to another registered dog. In that case, you must choose another name and resubmit the application. The sire and dam of the dog *must* have been registered to make the offspring eligible for registration. The AKC certificate is proof that your dog is purebred and registered as such with a recognized dog registry. A copy of this registration certificate may be required by the court if you are called to testify. *Never* release the original certificate unless you are giving up ownership of the dog.

The AKC, as well as several private businesses, can furnish you with a copy of your dog's pedigree. A pedigree lists the names of the sires and dams for a specified number of generations. A pedigree may also state which dogs were show champions and those that received an AKC title (such as a tracking or obedience title). At present the working abilities of search and rescue dogs are not recognized with a specific title by the AKC. A proposal to certify the Bloodhound is currently being developed by the American Bloodhound Club.

If the parentage of a dog is unknown it is possible to get an Indefinite Listing Privileged (ILP) number from the AKC. The number does not mean that your dog is guaranteed to be purebred but that the dog *appears* to be of pure stock. To get an ILP number the owner must submit photographs of the dog, statements, the AKC registration application and a fee. It may become an ILP requirement that the dog be spayed or neutered before an ILP number will be issued. It is important to note that an ILP number may not be recognized as valid in a courtroom at this time.

CANINE TRAINING RECORDS

A handler must maintain clear and accurate reports of all trails to establish and maintain credibility. Every training trail, demonstration or actual search requires a written report. Agencies that call dog teams may not require a handler to keep a detailed training log but I guarantee that the first time you are subpoenaed to a courtroom, if you don't keep records you will wish you had. The need for accurate and detailed training records may become painfully clear.

A good training record usually contains the following information:

A. Name of dog
B. Breed of dog
C. Age of dog when the trail was worked
D. Type of trail (purpose)
E. Date the trail was laid by the runner
F. Time the trail was laid by the runner
G. Terrain information
H. Weather information
I. Length of trail
J. Map drawn by runner
K. Date and time the dog was scented
L. Scent article description
M. Narrative of the dog's work
N. Weather when the trail was run
O. Disposition of the trail (find, etc.)
P. Distance covered by the dog
Q. Obstacles crossed by the dog
R. Problems
S. Time on trail
T. Handler's signature
U. Witnesses' (if any) signatures
V. Comments

The name, breed and age of the dog identifies the dog in question. Some handlers include coloring and sex as well.

Type of trail defines the specific type of training. A trail that has new obstacles, or one that is for obstacle training only, is different from a standard practice trail. Some different types of trails include: cadaver, line up, obstacle, demonstration, or education. Other types define the length or age of the trail. Trail types can also be based on the level of the dog's training, such as beginner, junior or senior status.

The date and time the trail is laid indicates the age of the trail when run. This information is especially useful in determining when a dog is ready to move on to older trails.

Terrain information establishes that you are continually changing the obstacles and areas that you are using for training. Using the same terrain for all practice trails severely limits a dog's working potential. Details in this section can specify the type of ground cover, vegetation, traffic, trees, wilderness, elevation, precipitation, or buildings found in the area.

The runner should write down the weather conditions when the trail was laid. This includes air temperature, ground conditions (wet, dry, snow), wind speed and wind direction. The record should indicate whether there was any noticeable precipitation when the trail was laid to help the handler determine scenting conditions and to understand a dog's reaction to a particular trail.

The length of the trail reflects the physical and scenting stamina of the dog. A beginner trail should be no more than one-half mile long. A junior level trail is no more than one mile long and a senior level trail should be no less than one and one-half miles long. Regulating the trail length confines the training into a reasonable area and reduces the chances that a dog will be overworked.

The runner must draw a map of the trail as he/she laid it to serve as a permanent record. The handler should not have access to the map until after the trail has been run, either successfully or unsuccessfully. As the team works the trail the judges mark the path of the team on the map. After the trail, the handler can see how the actual trail differed from what the dog did.

The scent article also is logged. A monthly review of training records can act as a reminder to continually vary the scent article used. By changing the type of article the handler can determine what works best for the dog on any given trail. Information on who chose the scent article and how it was chosen and packaged is also important.

Record the time it took for the dog to complete the trail, or the elapsed time from start to finish. If the handler pulls the dog off the trail or if the dog loses interest, this information and the handler's thoughts on why it happened should be included in the report.

A brief description is written to evaluate the dog on the trail. Include specific obstacles covered or problems encountered, whether the dog made a find or not, and any general observations that seem relevant.

SEARCH DOG TRAINING RECORD

DOG NAME	BREED	AGE	SEX	DOB
AKC#		CALL NAME	AKC#	
OWNED BY		HANDLED BY		

TYPE OF TRAIL

TYPE OF TRAINING	AGE OF TRAIL	LENGTH OF TRAIL
[ ] Beginner Trail (Line of sight/Hide and Seek)		
[ ] Intermediate Beginner Trail (Hide & Seek)		
[ ] Intermediate Trail (1-6 hrs old)		
[ ] Intermediate Advanced (6-12 hrs old)		
[ ] Advanced Intermediate (6 -12 hrs & 1 mile)		
[ ] Advanced (12 - 18 hrs)		
[ ] Pursuit Trail (1 mile or more)		
[ ] Locating evidence		
[ ] Physical obstacles, crossings		
[ ] Water crossings, water searches		
[ ] Trailing moving vehicles		
[ ] Cadaver Training (Source: _____)		
[ ] Line Up/Identification Trails		
[ ] Sterile Scent Article Trails (Article:_____)		
[ ] Advanced scenario trail (attach map & scenario)		

EVENT SPECIFICS

DATE TRAIL LAID	TIME	RUNNER NAME	SCENT ARTICLE
WIND SPEED & DIRECTION	TERRAIN	VEGETATION	AIR TEMPERATURE
PRECIPITATION	DESCRIPTION OF AREA		
DATE DOG STARTED	TIME	WIND SPEED & DIRECTION	AIR TEMP
PRECIPITATION	OBSTACLES	DISTRACTIONS/CONTAMINATION	

EVENT RESULT

[ ] DOG MADE FIND-UNASSISTED	[ ] DOG MADE FIND-ASSISTED (Re-scented)	[ ] DOG ALERTED-NO FIND
[ ] DOG RE-SCENTED-No Find	[ ] DOG RE-STARTED-No find	[ ] DOG CALLED OFF- by
[ ] DOG NEVER STARTED	[ ] OTHER	

Attach copies of all maps, scenarios, and related materials. MAKE SURE THE MAPS AND RECORDS ARE DATED!

HANDLER SIGNATURE _____ JUDGE SIGNATURE_____

If it takes the dog more than one hour to complete a trail one and one-half miles in length, I advise the handler to look closely at the path the dog worked. If the terrain was very difficult or if there were several obstacles, the handler should note this in the report. On the average, ninety minutes is more than enough time to work a trail that long. If it takes longer the handler should continue at this level until the dog can complete the trail in ninety minutes or less.

The handler must sign every training record, as should any witnesses present to lend credibility to the events.

Training records should also contain a map, drawn by the handler, detailing the work of the dog, specific locations where the dog crossed an obstacle or encountered a problem, and the path the dog took.

I recommend that handlers carry training record blanks in gear bags and complete the required record at the conclusion of a trail. Handlers that put off writing reports may forget key details. Training records must be legible and be signed. Some handlers have every training record notarized but this extreme is not necessary.

Training records should not be released to a third party. If an agency or court wants copies of specific training records the handler should make the copies. Avoid the possibility that the records become misplaced or destroyed by accident.

MISSION REPORTS

A mission report contains much more detail than a training record for the simple reason that an actual human life depended on the response of the dogs. A mission report has seven separate categories of information.

A. A section showing the date and location of the mission, name and phone number of the coordinator, and the base camp location.
B. A section detailing call-out and mileage information. This section should also include space to fill in the outcome of the mission.
C.. A section describing all information known about the search before going into the field, such as place, time and date last seen and scent article information.
D. A section listing specific information related to the missing person(s) including age, sex, and known medical problems. Any equipment they have with them and past experience with the activity is also helpful.

E. A section pertaining to the response effort including the name of each dog and the full name and emergency services worker number for each handler.
F. A narrative summary of the dog's activities on the trail. Street names, changes of direction and turns should be described as well as the approximate distance traveled. This section should include the search results, what team made the find, and the location and condition of the subject at the end of the search. Errors made by the dog or handler should also be recorded here.
G. A section listing any media present and obstacles or problems encountered.

The report must contain a signature line for the handler completing the report and space for the names of any witnesses. If possible get the mission coordinator's signature on your report. Have them sign as a witness after you have filled out your report.

Information in each section should be detailed but not excessively verbose. The one exception is the handler's narrative, which needs to be written in detailed prose. The form that we use consists of a series of boxes and blanks that are quickly completed at the scene. A different form is used for criminal or crime scene searches because the information is different.

As handlers, we will make mistakes and there will be times that we cannot believe what the dog appears to be telling us. Give your dog the benefit of the doubt—he is the expert.

I recall a search in which the underbrush was so dense that we were practically bouncing off it. I pulled Digger back and ended the trail there. We were transported to an area which we thought was located directly above where we had been stalled. Needless to say, Digger knew we were not in the same area and we ended up walking around for almost six miles. Later it was learned that the missing boys had been on the trail Digger worked four days before they got lost. The driver had assumed the distance instead of checking it and had dropped us almost a mile short of where we needed to be. In the mission report it clearly states "handler error."

MISSION REPORT			
MISSION DATE	CASE #	TYPE OF MISSION	COUNTY/STATE
TIME CALLED	AGENCY REQUESTING	CONTACT PERSON PHONE#	
DATE LEFT HOME	TIME	VEHICLE LICENSE#	ODOMETER READING
DATE ARRIVED AT SCENE	TIME	ODOMETER READING	
DATE ARRIVED HOME	TIME	ODOMETER READING	TOTAL MILES

SEARCH DATA			
SUBJECT NAME	AGE SEX	HEIGHT WEIGHT	
HOME ADDRESS	CITY STATE	PHONE	
OCCUPATION EXPERIENCE AT ACTIVITY	MEDICAL PROBLEMS/MEDICATIONS		
LAST SEEN WEARING	SHOE TREAD PATTERN		
EQUIPMENT TAKEN			
FOOD TAKEN	WHEN LAST ATE ALCOHOL/DRUGS?		
DATE LAST SEEN TIME	LOCATION	ACTIVITY/PLAN	

TRAIL INFORMATION

TYPE OF TERRAIN GROUND CONDITIONS   AIR TEMPERATURE   PRECIPITATION

VEGETATION AND TIMBER   WIND SPEED/DIRECTION   WEATHER SINCE LAST SEEN

DIRECTION OF TRAVEL   [ ] ROADS   [ ] TRAILS   [ ] CROSS COUNTRY
TYPE OF TERRAIN/OBSTACLES [ ] FLAT   [ ] STEEP   [ ] ROLLING   [ ] MTNS

TEAM INFORMATION

HANDLER NAME   DOG NAME   TOTAL HOURS   MILES

WORKING INFORMATION

DATE DOG STARTED   TIME   LOCATION

SCENT ARTICLE USED   COLLECTED FROM   BY

AGE OF TRAIL   TIME ON TRAIL   MILES WORKED

RESULTS

[ ] MADE INITIAL LOCATION OF PERSON UNASSISTED   [ ] WORKING TRAIL WHEN PERSON FOUND
[ ] HOUND OF NO ASSISTANCE   [ ] TRAIL WAS INCONCLUSIVE
[ ] PERSON NOT FOUND (Unknown disposition)   [ ] PERSON WALKED OUT ON THEIR OWN
[ ] EVIDENCE FOUND   [ ] DOG GAVE DIRECTION OF TRAVEL
[ ] TURNAROUND   [ ] OTHER

HANDLERS NARRATIVE: SHOULD BE WRITTEN ON THE BACK OF THIS FORM. ATTACH ALL MAPS AND OTHER INFORMATION!

In another case we took three qualified Bloodhounds to search for the driver of an abandoned car. The dogs went from an abandoned car to the river. It was a hot day and we had driven for two hours. When the dogs were urged to get to work they worked along the riverbank and then back up to the car and down the road. Digger trailed to the freeway. We later learned this was the route the subject had to use to get in or out of the area. When the dogs were started a second time they went into the river again and then up on the road, reluctantly. The river was not deep. Another handler and I walked the bank as far as we could and couldn't see anything. I requested that both the freeway and the river be checked but couldn't believe that a seventy-seven-year-old man would head down a river in the dark of night. The road was only ten feet from his car!

His body was found in the river, about a quarter of a mile below the car. The dogs had been right. In my report I credited the dogs with the right information and scored zero for the handlers. Believe your dog. Take advantage of your mistakes and use them to identify areas where more training would help to minimize the recurrence!

On criminal trails and on most regular searches I write a detailed narrative when I get home. I use a typewriter or the computer and put the original copy in my notebook with the search report. Remember that the more details you write down the more you will have to rely on should you need it later. Some questions you might pose include: Where and when was the person last seen and by whom? What was the plan and was the person to remain in one place? Is the person familiar with the area? What is the terrain like? Is there a trail or road, or is the trail going crosscountry? What is the weather like now and what was it like when the person disappeared? What have the wind and precipitation been like at the point last seen? Did the person disappear in daylight or after dark?

Determining the lifestyle of the missing person may help you establish the person's stamina and common sense in the field. Did the person walk or hike often? Were they on their feet at work? Did they eat regularly? Find out what kind of shoe the person was wearing as well as the tread. What size shoe did they wear? This will help you to identify the person's footprints in the event that you find some. Is the person on medication or does the person have any physical or emotional problems? Had there been an argument or any similar domestic problem? Is the person carrying a weapon? Does the person smoke, and if so, what brand and does he carry matches or a lighter? What was the direction of travel from the point last seen? Is there a favorite spot to which they might head?

A trailer and her Tracker. Vanna waits for the next trail.
PHOTO BY BETTY HENSLEE

Mission reports require more time and dedication, so be aggressive and obtain the necessary information before you leave the scene. Send a copy of your mission report to the agency that called you out. All of this information is required to verify your work if the case goes to court. It is also helpful if you are called back to continue to work on an unsolved case.

CRIMINAL REPORTS

When the dogs work in a crime scene or criminal search the chances of being called to the witness stand are almost guaranteed. Courtrooms are imposing places and court testimony can be a frightening experience for a new handler. The opposing attorney will go to great lengths to discredit you on the stand, but accurate and detailed records will provide the necessary proof to establish your credibility.

When handlers are called to testify, the attorney will request your training records. Allow the records to be copied and entered into the court records, but do not release the originals. Once an item is entered as evidence it remains in the custody of the court until the case is finished. If the case is appealed your records can be held for years.

The court may require the original records. If this happens you must provide them but it may be possible to bring the originals to the courtroom to be examined by the attorney and then to make a copy. Clearly explain that your hesitation to release the original records is based on the need to access the records for any other cases. Once the case report and mission summary have been turned in you may be released by the court if the dog evidence is uncontested. This means that you do not have to testify but it is always best to be prepared.

MEDIA RECORDS

If a media representative asks to follow you or begins to follow you as you work the dog, have someone stop them because it can be extremely distracting to have the media present while you are trying to work. Interviews and mock trails can easily be run when the work has been finished. Media representatives will usually wait until you finish the trail to talk with you since most media people would rather not lug video equipment through the brush at a high rate of speed. Get clearance from the coordinator and then arrange when and where you will contact them. Media representatives may dress like another searcher and can easily be mistaken for a member of another search group. Be careful what information you release to anyone. Get the permission of the mission coordinator before agreeing to interviews or releasing information about the mission. Conversations among searchers at base camp or over the radio, as monitored by a scanner, have appeared in the media because workers were not careful. Although this is not intentional, it may embarrass or anger the investigators or the team itself. Limit your radio traffic to only what is truly necessary. Consider every radio frequency accessible to the media and govern your radio conversations accordingly.

It should be noted that the media can also give you plenty of positive news coverage. My dogs have been on television, in regional magazines and in the newspaper a number of times. This kind of coverage is helpful in gaining acceptance.

Put copies of any articles or news reports concerning you or your dog team in your records. Add them to any written search report. Photographs, news articles and features are also helpful to track team exposure.

STORING RECORDS

Keep all of your reports in three-ring binders. Keep one notebook for training records and a separate notebook for mission reports. Choose a notebook that will hold about three inches of paper. The notebooks will keep the reports clean and in good shape through the years. Place copies of media coverage in envelopes and then place the envelope with the mission report it goes with. Store your notebooks in a cool, dry place.

Swamp Angel of Mercy.
ILLUSTRATION BY CRYSTAL MELVIN

CHAPTER FIVE

Field Training Basics

The training equipment sits ready, you have started the obedience training and now you feel the pull of the field. It's time to start training for your first search!

Training with your dog should begin as early as six weeks of age. I recommend starting a puppy within the first week in a new home after a few days of "orientation" and socialization. It is important to establish a training routine to help the dog get used to a training period and to work. Sporadic training efforts can reduce a dog's enthusiasm and create opportunities for failures and mistakes.

Keep the training sessions short and fun. The first week of training I spend fifteen minutes three times a day working with a puppy. The sessions are just a little bit longer if I am working an older dog. In the second and third week we work four times a day or, depending on the available time periods, we work for twenty minutes two or three times a day.

By the fourth week we are working thirty minutes twice a day. Be sure that the session is immediately followed by play-time and fun. I follow the fun time with a rest period before feeding my dogs because feeding a dog immediately after a workout can lead to bloat and torsion.

Once the dog has settled into its new home it is time to introduce him to the work equipment. The first step is to teach the dog to wear a collar and walk on a lead.

Start with a chain link, working collar. Choose a collar that is only 1"-2" longer than what is needed to go around the dog's neck. Be sure to put the collar on correctly so that it releases when the dog is compliant. Standing on the left side of the dog, take the collar in your hand and run one end through the other to make the collar loop. Hold the collar so that the ring the lead will clip onto is down and the collar makes a "P" shape. Place the collar over the dog's head so that the ring that snaps to the lead is at the top. When the lead is pulled it should tighten and when you loosen the lead the collar should loosen. Let the dog walk around with the collar on. Most likely he will try to rid himself of the collar by rolling on the ground, scratching at it or trying to rub it off.

Once the puppy has accepted the collar, attach the lead and allow the pup to drag it behind him. This may be frightening at first, but talking calmly and offering reassurance will make the transition easier. Pick up the end of the lead and while calling the dog by name, pull steadily. Praise the pup when he comes towards you and pull gently. Then allow the puppy to walk away from you and when the puppy reaches the end of the lead pull back gently but firmly and say "Easy!" This is to teach the puppy not to drag you along, which, if it becomes habit, is very hard to break.

Allow the puppy to acclimate to a harness without a collar or a lead. Most puppies will react to the sensation of the harness on their backs; the puppy may frantically roll and jump until he realizes that the harness won't hurt him and that he can't get it off. Then attach the lead and let the puppy lead you around. Remember to praise his efforts and, using the same "Easy!" command, continue to discourage any attempts to drag you along.

Some puppies and dogs are extremely frightened of a harness and it may take several attempts before he calms down. Be patient and praise good behavior. Add the collar and move the lead from the collar to the harness and back again so the pup gets used to the different sensations. When the lead is on the collar the puppy should know that *you* are in control. As you train the puppy to trail and track, the puppy will learn that when the lead moves from the collar to the harness, this is the signal to begin to work.

CHOOSING YOUR COMMANDS

Now it's time to choose your working commands. After basic obedience the most important command you will teach your dog is the one directing your dog to work. Each dog handler will need to establish their own starting command with the type of case determining which starting command is used. If you have more than one dog, be sure to use the same commands for each of them to minimize confusion.

I use "Find!" or "Find 'em!" to start a trail for a missing person. In the search for human remains I command the dogs to "Find Sam" which immediately tells them they are looking for a dead body. If the condition of the victim is undetermined, I will begin a search on the premise that the person is alive until we know otherwise. Some handlers use a foreign language for commands. A good friend of mine uses Swedish for his commands while another uses his Native American language. Choose something that you can remember.

Evidence searches and water searches necessitate still other commands. I use "Swim!" on water searches and "Check!" on evidence searches. When we pursue a criminal I use the word "Take!" One- or two-word working commands work best and try to make the commands different enough from each other to evoke a prompt response from the dog.

On one particular search Kady and I were working a trail to determine the direction that a murder suspect had taken after committing the crime. The area was inside the boundaries of a park and was heavily used by joggers and walkers. The site was wooded and crossed with many paths. I started Kady off with "Check!" and watched as she started working in a circle away from the body. She worked through some brush, stopped, turned around and then sat down. That was Kady's alert for finding evidence. I looked in the brush and saw a bloody butcher knife. Next to the knife was a bloody shirt shoved down partially under a bush and out of plain sight.

Kady then worked out of the brush, leading to a fence where a bloody handprint was found. Once we got over the fence Kady led to a gravel road and then to the paved street.

She started down the street working the berm on the side of the road until we were stopped by the detectives who told us that the suspect had been arrested just down the road from where we were standing. Kady had linked the crime scenes together!

When I was first starting out I was told *not* to talk to the dog while we were working because it would distract them. I tried that but found my dogs to be more encouraged by my talking with them, saying things like "Where did he go?" and "Where could he be?" as we moved along. As we move forward, recover evidence, or move through turns or changes in direction, I encourage and praise them. There are some situations including criminal pursuit work in which I talk very little since it may be dangerous to be talking while chasing a suspect. In those situations words are whispered and few. I use "Good dog!" and "Let's go!"

I added "Tunnel!" and "Crawl!" for recovery work; "Watch!" and "Wait!" were added for pursuit and criminal work as well as "Speak!" and "Climb!" As you develop your team it will be easy to select commands that you will need. Keep the commands simple and clear. I teach the dogs to stand still with the "Stand!" command whether it is used in the show ring or to stand still as I buckle on a rappelling harness that will lift us up into a helicopter or deposit us at a mission site. Some handler commands include, "Work!" "Search-Find!" "Search!" "Search Lost!" and "Where?!" The command should be simple and clear and one that will be used only in training or in a mission situation.

STARTING THE PUPPY

The first step in field training starts in the house or within the confines of your yard. As soon as the dog is accustomed to his new surroundings it is time to play hide and seek. Playing games with the dog is an excellent way to begin training as it immediately associates training with fun. Put the collar and harness on the puppy, walk away from him and try to hide. Praise the puppy for following and finding you. Distract the puppy with a toy to get the puppy to focus on the toy and not you. Leave and hide just out of sight of the puppy, around a corner or behind something, then call the puppy and wait.

If the puppy becomes frustrated and cries, call him. If he can't seem to figure out where you are, call him again or catch his attention by waving and then ducking down. Praise him for finding you. As he figures the game out make it more difficult. Have someone hold him back as you walk away, calling him, and disappear out of sight. Hide and then tell the holder to let the dog go. Call the pup once and wait. Again, lots of praise and pats for the successful puppy

Make sure the harness and collar are only on during working sessions. Take them off during playtime. Starting now you must keep written training records on *every* trail you work and every time you train.

Hide behind furniture, yard objects, doors, boxes or other objects. Make the game quick and fun in the beginning and gradually make it more difficult as the pup gets the hang of it. Move the game outside or to a bigger area. Once the puppy understands the game it is time to begin developing his skills by looking for strangers. You now move from being the quarry to being the handler.

Start the hide and seek game again but this time attach a lead to the puppy's collar. Have the runner walk away, calling the puppy and stepping out of sight. Move the lead from the collar to the harness and give the puppy the "Find!" command. Release the tension on the lead and let the puppy go after the runner. If the puppy doesn't start searching have the runner call him. When the pup moves forward give him the working command again and encourage him. Don't pull or steer him with the lead, just keep it slack.

If the pup stops or gets distracted have the runner call him and make sure that the runner gives the puppy a treat or lots of attention when the pup makes the find. Make sure it is a big deal so the puppy is willing to try again! Puppy trails should include some trails where the person is within the line of sight of the puppy but further away so that all the puppy has to do is run to them. Mix in some hidden runner trails but keep things fun and consistent. Be sure to start each trail with the command to work and encourage the dog along the way.

Ben started out eagerly finding his runners. When he had been in training for about a month a new runner, Nick, started working with us. Nick was well over 6' 6" tall and because of his size Ben was a little unsure of him. To get Ben to go up to Nick without shying away, Nick started out lying on the ground and Ben would run up to Nick wiggling and wagging. Slowly Nick began "growing," changing his position from lying on the ground to being up on his elbows, hands and knees, kneeling, crouching and finally standing. By the time Nick was standing and hiding Ben would trot right up to Nick and crawl into his lap! Remember to take things slowly and watch for areas indicating that you need to slow down and work through a training issue like just as Ben did.

Once the dog understands that he is to find the runner, gently introduce a scent article. I start doing this passively by having the runner drop a T-shirt or cap or jacket as they walk away, to serve as a part of the trail but something that is rich with the scent of the runner. The dog should not be allowed to get distracted and play with the item but should be encouraged to sniff it and move along. I start with the article at about the midpoint of the trail and then have the runner vary where it is dropped.

One of the biggest stumbling blocks for a working dog is to have a handler that steers or guides the dog by using pressure on the lead. Remember that you are learning to follow the dog who is following scent, something you cannot see. You have to learn to trust the dog. In these early stages watch the path the runner takes, the jogs and the turns, and then watch the pup as he follows. Notice how closely he follows the trail and watch his body language. You will be learning the dog's signals and how he may operate in the field.

Kady would signal turns and changes in the trail by changing the way she held her tail. This is very common. When the dog is on trail and working, the tail is held up; in areas of contamination or areas where there is a scent pool the tail drops to half-mast. Once the dog picks up the trail the tail goes back up and if the trail ends suddenly the tail drops. If the dog comes across a body or detects fear the tail drops and curls under the dog. Some handlers refer to these tail movements as *alerts* or *flags*. Get to know how your dog signals trail changes.

YOUR FIRST TRAILS

The first trails should be no more than ten yards long. Keep them short and fun and as the dog masters the trails, add the passive scent article. Add a turn or have the runner hide under a box or behind the door so that the dog has to show you where the runner is.

Look at how you are pacing the dog on the trail. The dog should work at a brisk pace but not a dead run. Hastiness contributes to missing turns and losing trails and it can be very dangerous as well. Running pell mell behind a dog in the dark can result in tragedy. When I was much younger and when Digger was a pup, we were both so excited to work that we would run. It looks impressive but the problems started as Digger grew bigger and more powerful—he could run for long distances but I couldn't. Once we fell down a steep embankment while searching late one night. I ended up breaking my tailbone on a stump and both of us were quite shaken up. Gradually we learned to slow down.

The other problem is that Bloodhounds do not work a straight trail. They work side to side, crossing back and forth in front of you. You have to pay attention to avoid colliding with the dog or being knocked down. Bloodhounds are athletes who should be kept in good condition, but there are few distance runners that will run behind one of my hounds. One of my corrections officers was a distance runner and a fan of the Bloodhounds. He offered to take Digger running to keep him in shape. Although I wasn't sure if he meant to keep himself in shape or Digger, I agreed, knowing that this running partnership wouldn't last long. The guy took Digger running once. They weren't gone very long when I heard him hit the porch, literally. I looked out to see my friend soaking wet, scraped knees and hands, wet and filthy dirty. Digger had loved the chance to go for a run. This poor guy had fallen a number of times trying to avoid running into Digger. Digger meanwhile had enjoyed the nice run, sniffing back and forth along the road, down into the irrigation ditch and back up to the road. My friend never offered to take Digger for a run again.

The start of the trail. PHOTO BY KAY SCHMITT

Field experience has taught me that trails can suddenly disappear over a cliff, down a mine shaft, off a pier, onto the freeway or into the path of a bullet. A running dog and handler can easily stumble and fall, becoming more of a hindrance to a search than a help. Hazards on the trail are inevitable, but control and training may avert some dangers.

Beginning dogs are very prone to getting overly excited and missing turns or overrunning the trail in their eagerness to find the person on the other end. This is very normal and can be easily controlled. If the dog misses a turn let the runner call the dog once. When the dog stops and turns in the direction of the call, encourage him to "Find!" If the dog continues in the wrong direction take him back to where he missed the turn or overran the trail and again have the runner call the dog. Re-command him to "Find!" and encourage him to work. You may

Across grass, dirt and gravel. Photo by Kay Schmitt

be allowing the dog to move too fast, so stop, regroup and go back to the start, slowing things down until the dog hits the turns. If the dog still misses the turn have the runner drop an article at the turn or just before it for a couple trails, but don't make this kind of assistance a habit or the dog will look for such signals on future trails.

As the dog gains confidence and as you learn to identify the working pattern of the dog, move the practice outside and to a larger area. Gradually make the trail more difficult, slowly increasing the ten-yard trail to one hundred yards and adding variables like brush or other kinds of natural cover for the runner.

Choose only one variable at a time. Lengthen the trail distance or the age of the trail or add an obstacle, but remember to make changes in small increments. One handler came to me for help, explaining that he was frustrated because his dog was

Following the invisible path. Photo by Kay Schmitt

not making it to the end of the training trails. The dog would lose the trail and start goofing off instead of working and the handler was strongly considering getting a new dog. He felt that this one apparently didn't "have what it takes" to stick with a trail.

In talking further with the handler I learned that the dog had, in fact, been doing really well, eagerly working trails that were up to a quarter-mile long and fifteen minutes old. The handler had instructed the runner to lay trails more than one-half mile long and he had aged the trails to at least four hours in one training session. Suddenly the fresh tracks were twice as long and sixteen times as old! It's no wonder the dog was having trouble!

I laid a trail that was one hundred yards long and had the handler wait fifteen minutes. The dog worked the trail without hesitation. We added two turns and fifty more yards to the

Found by the Hound! PHOTO BY JAN TWEEDIE

next trail. The dog handled that well. Over the next several days distance was the primary obstacle. Once the dog was doing well on fresh trails up to three-quarters of a mile long we went back to a shorter trail but started aging the trails.

The first trail was one hundred yards long but thirty minutes old. The next trail was one hundred yards long, had one turn and was forty-five minutes old, then an hour old, and so on. Once I showed him how to work on only one variable at a time, the dog consistently worked trail after trail. In less than a week the dog was working a trail over a mile long and an hour old and by the second week the dog was working trails that were more than two miles long and four hours old. A year or so later I happened to sit in on a training session this particular handler was teaching and heard him drilling his students in controlling variables and encouraging consistency.

Learn from your mistakes. Remember that you are trying to create a reliable, flexible search partner, so make sure your training is consistent and your targets are achievable. Keep track of all changes by noting them on your training records.

I prefer to increase the trail distance before I age the trail. Don't change anything until the dog is working a specific trail problem successfully on a consistent basis. If the dog runs a fifty-yard trail with no problem in ten different situations he is ready to move on to a new variable. I usually lengthen the trail first. Be careful to choose short lengths first. Use increments of one quarter mile for distance and fifteen-minute time intervals for the novice dog. Once the dog is working well we increase to thirty-minute intervals until the trail is aged two hours, then in one-hour blocks until the trail is four hours old.

After you are working trails that are one-half mile to one mile long, you can move in one-half-mile lengths to a distance of three to five miles. Increase the age of the trails in two- to four-hour blocks until the trail is six to eight hours old. Then move in four- to eight-hour blocks to trails that are twenty-four hours old. Then use twelve-hour intervals to age the trails. After the dog is working trails that are four hours old you should feel confident in moving ahead. Remember to change only one variable at a time.

A typical training schedule and progression consists of trails from Table 5-1. The trails are worked in the order presented until the dog has been successful in finding the runner five times consecutively, and only then do we move to the next level of difficulty.

As the dog progresses remember to add obstacles such as turns, road crossings, creeks, or crossing runners. If the dog starts having difficulty, go back to the last exercise at which the dog was successful and repeat it. Review your training records. I also recommend that you review fresh short trails on a regular basis. If you quit practicing fresh trails your dog will tend to ignore fresh scent and look for the older, more settled scent and you will be of no use in looking for people who are recently missing!

How long should it take for the dog to work the trail and make his find? It is generally accepted that some dogs work

Table 5-1

TYPE	TRAIL LENGTH	TRAIL AGE
Puppy	30 feet	Fresh (hide and seek)
Puppy	50 feet	Fresh (hide and seek)
Puppy	100 feet	Fresh (hide and seek)
Puppy	100 feet	10, 15, and 30 minutes
Puppy	150 feet	10, 15, and 30 minutes
Puppy	200 feet	15, 20, and 30 minutes
Novice Beginner	100 yards	30, 45, and 60 minutes
Novice Beginner	200 yards	30, 45, and 60 minutes
Novice Beginner	300 yards	30, 45, and 60 minutes
Novice Beginner	300 yards	90 and 120 minutes
Beginner	400 yards	2 and 3 hours
Beginner	1/4 mile	2 and 3 hours
Beginner	1/4 mile	3 and 4 hours
Intermediate Beginner	1/2 mile	1, 2, and 4 hours
Intermediate Beginner	1/2 mile	4, 6, and 8 hours
Intermediate	1/2 mile	8, 12, and 24 hours
Intermediate	3/4 mile	2, 4, and 8 hours
Intermediate	3/4 mile	12 and 24 hours
Intermediate	1 mile	4, 8, 12, and 24 hours
Intermediate	1 1/2 mile	8, 12, and 24 hours

more slowly and methodically while others move more quickly. On the average, a dog should take no more than two hours to work a trail that is one and one-half miles long and twenty-four hours old on mild terrain or in mild conditions after consistent training. If it takes longer I recommend that you back up, review and spend more time training. Are your trails too complicated? Closely examine the obstacles you are using and practice, practice, practice!

Remember that you are training your hound to deal with distance, age and obstacles on the way to finding the right person.

In the beginning practice towards that goal, without adding the pressure of the clock. You will telegraph your feelings of anger and frustration down the lead to the dog and those emotions become obstacles for both you and the dog. Let the dog work at his own speed until he is consistent, then pay attention to the time it takes him to get there. Different training issues take time to work out; if necessary ask an experienced handler for help.

RUNNERS

As you train the dog vary the person who lays the trails. Using the same runner may condition the dog into believing that the goal is not serious since the runners are always found or come home on their own anyway. Use people that are strangers to the dog as often as possible.

Rook was an enthusiastic owner of a new Bloodhound puppy. The puppy eagerly accepted the harness and they started training using Rook's daughter Haley as the runner. The dog was around the child all day long and after the newness of the hide and seek game wore off the pup began to wander and follow other scents instead of looking for Haley. After a month the pup's dedication to the trail wavered.

Rook tried giving Haley treats to carry and the pup would start searching eagerly, but then begin to wander. Rook tried guiding the puppy to Haley but the pup would take the treat and then immediately begin sniffing around following other scents. Rook called me in frustration because he felt that the pup didn't have the instinct to trail.

I invited Rook to meet me at the park down the road from his house and I spent a few minutes looking the puppy over, playing with him and showing him the piece of raw liver I had brought. I put the puppy down and I laid a trail and Rook harnessed him and told the puppy to "Work!" The puppy sniffed around the jacket I left on the ground at the start, his tail went up, his head went down and he eagerly started working. He followed the trail through the grass, around the swings, across a gravel path and into the brush to my feet. He wagged and wiggled and gobbled the liver, whining the whole time.

I had Haley lay a quick trail and handed her a piece of the liver, which she reluctantly took. The pup sniffed Haley's hat lying on the ground and then turned in the opposite direction, happily heading for me. I asked a boy playing in the park to lay a trail parallel to Haley's and the pup trailed him. The pup then trailed two other kids in the park, trailed me again and then trailed Rook with me handling him.

I think that the pup knew Haley wouldn't go too far. He knew she would go home with them and he knew he could find her anytime. He didn't know me or the others and he also knew that I had some great treats so he trailed us eagerly. I told Rook that I thought the pup had figured the game out pretty well and I encouraged him to vary his runners teaching the pup to look for whomever Rook wanted.

It may be difficult to find people willing to lay trails over and over. Try your local Scout troops, Boys and Girls Clubs, Little League team, neighborhood kids, Orienteering Club or Search and Rescue groups including Explorer Search and Rescue and the local Civil Air Patrol Squadron. As you make contact with local civic groups, try asking them to help out.

Be sure to carefully explain what you want the runner to do. Go so far as to draw a map of the trail you want them to run, telling them not to vary anywhere unless you approve it. Only when you have built up trust in your dog should you consider allowing a runner to improvise trail elements.

Improvising a trail too early interrupts the learning process. If you are expecting the trail to go one way and the dog goes another, it will be confusing for both of you when you stop the dog or try to control him. If this happens, make notes of where the dog responds differently than expected. Then check with your runner and find out how these responses correlate with how and where the trail was changed. Check your notes to see if you caught the changes in the dog where the trail was varied. Did you try to steer or guide the dog to where you believed the trail went? Did you give up, knowing you were right because the runner was told not to change the trail? You have to expect to train runners as well as the dog and yourself! Even with mistakes, patiently observing and taking good notes can teach you a lot about how your dog works.

Vary your runners. Should you run trails on more than one runner in the same day? Yes. In the same training session? Yes, you should be able to. If the dog falters, back up and review. Run trails on one runner for a few days, then change runners. Slowly work up to two trails with two different runners. Remember that changing runners is an obstacle in training. Be sure to account for those variables as you plan your training. As the ability of the dog and handler increases, the confidence increases and working the dog becomes more natural. Don't rush the dog through training sessions. Don't move on to the next level before your dog shows proficiency on the current level.

MORE ABOUT ALERTS

A dog's tail carriage and body language are its method of communicating to you and you will learn vital information about the trail. Experienced handlers can usually tell when the dog is working on a fresh scent, an old scent, working through a scent pool, working through a contaminated area or when the dog has lost the trail. Each dog is different and experienced handlers have to spend time working with new dogs to learn how they will signal.

Digger worked with his tail up and the closer he got to a live person the faster he worked, his tail beginning to wag. Kady held her tail up and still as she approached a find and Jethro began to "sing" and whine as he made his approach. Swamp Angel was more subtle, holding her tail about three-quarters up and wagging it in subtle circles.

As the hounds approach a dead body their body language often becomes more subdued, almost sad. Digger, Swamp Angel and Ben would slow down, tails drooping, while Kady would get more intense and snort. Some hounds whine and bay as they approach a body while others carry their tails high over their back. If the trail is lost, the dog's tail may drop, and some dogs begin to work in a circle or back and forth in an effort to locate the scent.

Some dogs alert very obviously. When the dog is frightened and crawls underneath the table or dives behind you, that is an obvious alert. The dog may drop his head and tail when you scold him and that is also a kind of alert. Other behavior is much more subtle and will require careful attention to interpret. You must be generally familiar with alert patterns to learn to read the dog and it takes time and a concerted effort.

Each dog deals with the scent article differently as well. Digger would deliberately sniff and push on the article while Kady and Ben sniffed at it and moved away almost immediately. As you train, watch the way the dog chooses to use the article. If the dog just whiffs the article but finds the runner, it would appear that the quick whiff is all he needs. On the other hand, if the dog misses the trail or ignores the scent article you probably need to work on this in training.

As you work your dog take note of his behavior. How does he react to the runners taking off? Does he wag his tail when he greets them? How does he react to the scent article? Does he pick it up? Does he miss it? Try putting the article in a bag and see if the dog checks inside the bag. When you give the working command does the dog's tail come up? Does the dog circle and then take off? What does he do with his tail when he has the scent? Watch his body language as he approaches and makes turns, or overshoots a turn. What does he do as he closes in on and then finds the runner? All of these clues will help you as you learn how to read your dog.

USING MARKED TRAILS

Another way to discover how your dog responds to the trail is to create a marked trail. Using grid ribbon, toilet paper or a similar material, have the runner mark the start, all turns and changes of direction, locations where the trail crosses a creek or another path, where other people cross the trail and the end of the trail. Have the runner put the markers at eye level for the handler and as you approach a marker, watch the dog's body language and any changes in the way he moves or works.

I will use a flagged trail to help a handler learn to identify the alerts. I use three different colors of tape; one color indicates the start and finish, another color indicates turns and changes in direction and a third color may indicate scent pools or nothing at all. I watch both the dog and the handler for alerts. I do not tell the handler what the various colors mean and often the handler will alert and try to anticipate a turn or guide the dog to slow down or check. Be aware that this method can increase the chances that a handler will guide the dog instead of trusting him.

Keep in mind that this method is intended to help *you* learn to read your dog. Use marked trails periodically to check your progress but don't become dependent on them. Other than Hansel and Gretel there are few lost persons who will flag their trail in the wilderness!

TRAINING PITFALLS AND PLATEAUS

You and your dog are working well together, the dog is trailing his heart out and successful trails are the norm. Suddenly and unexplainably the dog can't handle even the simplest trails. What is happening?

Going backwards and hitting performance plateaus are to be expected. One of the key reasons to vary your training and to include regular reviews is to help limit these occurrences. Go back and cover shorter distances and fresher trails, use contaminated scent articles or multiple runners or crossing runners and refresh your understanding of your dog's alert signals and body language. Reviewing various skills helps to reinforce the building blocks and prepares the team for new training.

Patrick and Julie Cardinal each had dogs in training and both were doing well. It didn't take long before both Zipper and Tory were working trails that were at least one and one-half miles long and twenty-four hours old. The SAR group they were part of required that each dog work three trails of that length and age before they would qualify to respond to actual missions. On Zipper's first "official" try he garnered his first qualifying trail. Soon Tory nailed her first required trail and quickly had the second qualifier. Zipper picked up his second qualifier later in the following month.

Left: Which way?
PHOTO © DEBORAH PEARCY

Below:
Searching on pavement.
PHOTO © DEBORAH PEARCY

Bottom:
Into the
brush.
PHOTO
© DEBORAH
PEARCY

At a special event, Patrick and Julie entered both dogs, confident that they could pick up the third and final qualifying trail. They went out the first day and both failed to locate their runner. They tried again the next day and again both dogs failed. Julie and Patrick were tired, frustrated, angry and confused. The dogs did so well in training, and conditions and terrain were the same as they practiced in. Why couldn't they work this one trail?

Sometimes a number of variables can factor into a dog's performance. Ask yourself some questions to try to isolate the problem areas. Is the trail too difficult? Is the weather playing a part? Why? Was the dog at fault or the handler? Was it the runner or the trail or the site? Was it the terrain or the weather? Were the judges jerking them around? Had they been set up? Were the trails laid right? Could it have been a bad scent article? Was the map drawn incorrectly by the runner? Is the runner confused? What kind of animals live around the area? Are they confusing or distracting the dog? Are there human paths crossing the trail?

Train in poor weather and at night as well as in the daylight under good conditions to prepare you for the actual missions. Get used to wearing a headlamp and using it at night. Have your runners plot their trail on a map and become familiar with reading maps. Work on crime scene scenarios in training and learn to map your trail in a criminal or "normal" search situation.

If your dog fails to start working, look at the scent article, the terrain and the starting point environment at the search site. Are there a number of people standing around? Are there stray dogs in the area? Is there a police canine barking nearby? Are there vehicles parked and running in the starting area contaminating the scene with exhaust fumes? Does the dog start trailing from the scent article to a bystander? Did the bystander collect or contaminate the article? Is someone standing there eating? Does the trail move along a waterway and then suddenly stop? Have you practiced working across a creek? Does the dog stop at a fence and not move on? Have you worked on getting the dog over or around the fence and back to the right spot? Did you flag the point on the fence to which you need to return?

Bad experiences can permanently affect your dog and you. If your dog is attacked by another dog while he works he may shy away from or cease working in the presence of other dogs. Gunfire, thunder, loud crashing noises and similar sounds can frighten and freeze your hound. Practice working around distracting noises, but be sure that the hound feels safe. Honking horns, barking dogs, crashing garbage cans, motorcycles, lawn mowers and similar noises can all be worked into your practice runs.

Training a dog with constant variety will focus a dog on his goal. It is truly a challenge to keep inventing twists in the training. I have runners who will climb fences, swim creeks and rivers, jump off piers, crawl inside barrels and caves and hide under boards and debris. A few runners will cut through swamps or bogs. Others will hide in the trunk of a car and be driven down the road. Still others will lay a trail and then wait at the end in the depths of winter. Simulated plane crashes with wandering victims, drunks who wander away from wrecked cars and crazed suspects running from crime scenes all become training scenarios I use to keep things moving.

I also vary the search site. We may work on searching barns or outbuildings, looking for people in office buildings with floors that are carpeted or covered with slick linoleum. We also take rides on small planes, in helicopters, tractors and snowmobiles. We train in the heat, the rain, the wind and the snow. We train at night, start at dawn or work all day. Orchards, vineyards, pastures, corrals, parking lots and malls all become mission sites.

Every handler has hit a performance plateau or has had to step back, review and retrain. It is natural and a part of working a dog. I look forward to reviewing and practicing things again as an opportunity to build confidence and add on to the training foundation. Try to use these experiences as building blocks, *not* stumbling blocks!

CREATING MORE ADVANCED
TRAINING SITUATIONS

After the dog has mastered the fresh "pursuit" trail as well as the twenty-four to thirty-six hour old trails, and when he can work for at least two miles to a find, you are ready to move on to tougher training situations.

DROP TRAILING

Drop trailing involves using a vehicle for either the runner or the dog or both. Your dog must be confident working along a road and not be shy of moving vehicles. Have the runner lay a trail out to a road that has a shoulder of grass or dirt. Have them turn right or left, go down the road ten to twenty yards and then hide. Start the dog on a shorter lead to protect him from traffic, if necessary. Make the first few trails short and easy to build the confidence of both dog and handler. Once the dog has mastered this, the runner should move down the road, crossing it from time to time or walking down the shoulder and back up to the road.

Next have the runner start down the road and then have him get picked up in a car. Have the runner sit on the passenger side of the car with the window down. The scent will blow off the runner riding in the car and land along the roadway. Every hundred yards or so stop the car and have the runner get out, create a scent pool, run down the road, get back in the car and move further down the road. The runner can end the trail hiding in the car out of sight, or hiding in the brush near the car or continue the trail on foot hiding off the road.

You can advance your drop trailing experience by sending the runner out with a driver to lay the trail. Have them use a road with several intersections and instruct the runner to get out at the second or third intersection and turn right onto the new road and wait in the car. Start the dog along the road and then load him into a car. Leave the lead attached to the harness because the dog is still working. Stop the car at least fifty yards before the intersection, get the dog out and re-command him to work. You may have to re-scent him the first time or two. Let the dog work the trail to the intersection to tell you if the runner continued on or turned. When the dog finds the car encourage him to check the car out, even get into the car to find the runner.

Increase the difficulty gradually, moving the trail across the road, rolling the window up a little more each time, or hiding the runner in the trunk or under a tarp or box at the end of the trail. Have the runner leave the car door open and move away from the vehicle to hide so that the dog will have to work through and away from the scent pool to find the runner.

If the dog cannot seem to work away from the vehicle after significant effort you may need to help him. Put the lead back on his collar, walk him away from the vehicle and re-command him to work. The physical distance of just a few feet may be enough to get him back to work. Practice and patience will develop the required skills to link patches of scent together forming a path to the runner.

These skills help build the dog's problem-solving skills and encourage the dog to work in the midst of distractions like moving vehicles and working on different surfaces like gravel roads, berms, asphalt, concrete and grass.

I use the "victim-in-the-trunk" scenario to train criminal search teams. Other variables for vehicle work include moving the runner around in the car and rolling a window down on the side of the car opposite the runner. Few vehicles, if any, are truly airtight and scent will flow out of vents and frame spaces. The final challenge could be placing a runner in the vehicle under a blanket with all windows rolled up. Progressing to the most advanced stages takes time and lots of practice. Don't rush.

Remember that you are responsible for the safety of the people with whom you are working. Be sure that no one is ever locked in a trunk and don't hide in trunks on hot days. If you are interested in how your dog will respond to a person in a trunk, park the vehicle in a garage or in a cool location so that your runner doesn't overheat. Remember that the road surfaces can get extremely hot and can easily burn a dog's feet. Consider the health and safety of all of your two- and four-legged partners!

TROUBLESHOOTING

If you encounter a problem in the field, incorporate a similar situation into your training routine to work on a variety of ways to deal with it. Every dog and handler will have bad days when it seems everything learned has been forgotten. Murphy's Law affects everything. The most frustrating thing is that the dog and handler never seem to have the same bad day! There will be times that the dog just can't or won't get started. You may be stiff and sore or sick. Your equipment may break down. You may be working against insurmountable mission elements such as no scent article, no starting point, poor weather, rough terrain, and not being called out soon enough or at all. Some of those frustrations are training issues—other things are out of your control.

A police officer was working his dog searching for evidence in a rape case. The dog trailed to a six-foot cyclone fence and stopped, obviously interested in the continuing the trail, but the dog couldn't get over or under the fence. The dog dug at the bottom of the fence. The handler gave the dog an "Out!" command, unharnessed the dog and walked the dog down the fence until he found a way through. He re-harnessed the dog on the other side and re-commanded the dog to start working. The dog turned and looked at him, sniffed around the ground and rolled in the grass. The handler forced the dog back up and along the fence repeatedly commanding her to get to work. The handler decided the dog was done working and he was going to walk the dog back to the car when suddenly the dog jerked him off his feet and began dragging him away from the fence appearing to be working her trail. He let her continue and she trailed away from the fence, across a road and to a building, locating evidence inside. Afterwards the handler went back to the point on the fence where the dog had picked up the trail. When he looked through to the other side of the fence he could see where she had dug in the ground trying to get under the fence.

He had chosen the starting point on the other side where the dog couldn't pick up a trail. The point he chose was more than one hundred yards off from the actual trail. Even though the handler had given the "Out!" command, the hound could not resist picking up the right trail when she had a chance.

It is important to include breaks in the trail, water stops and similar distractions to your practice sessions so that you can work past them in the field. Does your dog have a difficult time restarting after you take a break? Does the hound struggle with working through or out of scent pools? They have to be exposed to them in practice! Practice trailing to a fence and having to go to a gate. Mark the fence with grid tape or a marker to show you where you need to return to re-start. Learn to lift your dog over obstacles. Teach your dog to allow others to lift it over fences.

Prepare for missions by exposing the dog to distractions and obstacles. Run trails through neighborhoods where dogs are loose. How will you deal with a stray or loose dog following you or challenging your hound?

SCENT ARTICLES

Millions of dead skin cells are shedding off a person's body every minute, landing on nearby articles or carried on the air currents, forming scent. A scent article is an item of clothing or an article that the missing person touched or wore. Scent articles come in a variety of forms but the basic items are articles of clothing which have not been laundered and which were recently worn by the missing person.

A second category includes scents that the dog obtains from a car seat, chair, a wallet or some other personal item, such as a bed sheet or a pillowcase.

Gathering advanced scent articles involves using gauze or paper towels to wipe scent from a known entry point, from the clothing of a victim, as in the case of a criminal pursuit, and from evidence left at the scene or dumped along the way.

When referring to scent articles, it is easier to classify them by the ease with which a clean scent of the person can be obtained:

Simple scent article — These items include clothing worn recently (within the past twenty-four to forty-eight hours) by the missing person. This clothing cannot have been laundered or mixed with other people's clothing nor can it have been touched by anyone prior to the arrival of the handler. The fitted bottom sheet or the pillowcase from the victim's bed makes an effective scent article.

Marginal scent articles — These items include the victim's wallet or purse, car seat, drinking cup, or similar item that may have been contaminated by other people. These include articles collected by officers or others at your direction, possibly packaged in used bags. The articles are considered contaminated.

Complex scent articles — These items include weapons, evidence, or an item found exposed to the elements which requires using gauze or paper towels to absorb the scent. Human blood is a complex scent article. This category also includes points of entry or exit, victim's clothing that may have been handled, or crime scene articles in a criminal pursuit, including footprints.

Some items are not as likely to hold scent as others, resulting in great scent articles, good scent articles, marginal scent articles, and contaminated or useless scent articles.

Examples of a great scent article include uncontaminated clothing (preferably a T-shirt, pants, jacket, hat, or gloves), a bed sheet or pillowcase, sleeping bag, vehicle, or suitcase with worn clothing in it. As long as the item has been secured and is uncontaminated, it is considered a great scent article.

A good scent article includes footprints that are discovered away from the point last seen and which are uncontaminated by other searchers, or clothing that has been handled only by the handler and one other person who is present at the point from which the dog will be started.

A marginal scent article is any item which may have been or is known to have been contaminated by more than one person at the scene or that was possibly laundered or located in a contaminated area.

A useless scent article is any item that has been handled by more than two people (one of whom is the handler) when

Collect a scent article using a tool such as a wooden spoon.
Don't stand over the article as you collect it.
PHOTO BY JAN TWEEDIE

the person who contaminated the scent article is no longer present. Other articles in this category include anything that cannot be positively identified as belonging to or having been worn by the missing person or that has been exposed to the elements, contaminated by chemicals (fingerprint powder) or that has been stored in a deodorized bag.

SELECTING AND COLLECTING YOUR SCENT ARTICLE

Selection of the scent article is best left to the handler. The handler knows the dog and knows the dog's ability to detect and hold a scent and work around contamination problems. Avoid using underclothing and socks as scent articles because underpants absorb moisture and will smell more of urine, which may confuse the dog. Socks absorb the smell of the shoes, and leather shoes distort the scent the dog will be following.

If the handler is able to select his own scent article from the residence of the missing person, the best place to isolate and bag the scent article is in the bedroom. Stay away from

Hold the sack by the outside.
PHOTO BY JAN TWEEDIE

community laundry hampers because the scent of anyone else using that hamper will be intermingled and will be confusing to the dog.

Once you arrive in the bedroom, take a good look around. Was the person neat and tidy? Was everything put away? Was there any sign of a struggle (are things knocked over, or is there blood anywhere)? Is the missing person the sole occupant of the bedroom? If so and if no one has gone through the clothing, it would be safe to isolate an item of clothing that appears to have been worn or that is known to have been worn like nightclothes or a bathrobe. If there is any doubt, remove the bottom fitted sheet and the pillowcase and bag them separately.

To remove a pillowcase, grab the bottom of the case (the sewed end) with an inverted bag over your hand (use a medium-sized bag for this). Shake the pillow out of the case until it can be pulled out without touching the case or the bag. Push the inverted bag over the scent article until you have it encased in the bag; then seal the bag or twist the top until you are ready to start your trail.

Once the item has been bagged, make sure the bag opening has been closed. Paper bags should be rolled from the top to seal the item in; plastic bags should be twisted and taped or tied if possible; *Ziploc* bags have natural seals which are closed quickly and easily.

If the only scent article available is a vehicle and you can isolate where the missing person was seated most recently, you will need to bring out scent collection materials.

A scent collection kit consists of sterile gauze pads (4"x4") or paper towels that you have picked up in a sterile manner by carefully by inverting the bag over your hand without touching the inside of the bag. Seal the bag without touching the contents or bag. The sterile prepackaged pads are best. You will need deionized or distilled water and gallon-sized *Ziploc* bags or un-deodorized plastic garbage bags. A number of new lunch sacks or small new paper grocery sacks are also useful.

A recently fired weapon is not usually considered a good scent article because of the overwhelming scent of gunpowder. The scent article is collected from the grips.
PHOTO BY JAN TWEEDIE

Scent Article Collection Kits

General Scent Article Collection Kit

Container (duffel bag)
Paper bags—12 large
Paper bags—12 small
Ziploc bags—12 large
Ziploc bags—12 medium
Ziploc bags—12 small

Gloves—6 pair disposable
Distilled water—1 quart
Tongs—1 pair standard size
Wooden spoon—1 large
Plastic bags—12 large
Envelopes—12 medium

Sterile Scent Article Collection Kit

Paper bags—large, 6 standard grocery size (new)
Plastic bags—12 standard non-deodorized lawn size
Paper bags—small, 6 standard lunch size (new)
Forceps—1 pair
Gloves—rubber, 6 pair
Index cards—12 small
Tongs—1 pair
Ziploc bags—large, 24 1-gallon size
Ziploc bags—small, 12 sandwich size

Gauze pads—24 sterile 2" x 2"
Hemostats—1 pair locking type
Pen—1
Distilled water—1 quart
Ziploc bags—medium, 12 1-qt size

Using your scent collection gauze (and without directly touching the bag or the gauze), dampen the gauze with the distilled water and wring it out. Run the damp gauze over the seat, door handle or steering wheel to collect the scent. Try to wipe only 50% of the area that contains the victim's scent so that you can collect at least two scent articles. Seal the bag until you are ready to begin your trail.

To collect scent from a window ledge, door frame, or other point of entry or exit, you will also need to use a collection kit. Using the same method to dampen the gauze without touching it, wipe the gauze over the door frame, ledge or furniture with which the suspect made contact. Seal the bag until you are ready to work the trail.

Using sterile pad and an inverted bag, a sterile scent article is collected from the windowsill where an intruder has crossed. The pad is drawn back into the bag to be used as a scent article for the dog.

PHOTO BY JAN TWEEDIE

Commonly Used Scent Articles

Shirt	T-shirt	Pants
Jacket	Car seat	Pillowcase
Sheet	Gloves	Hat
Wallet	Scarf	Footprint
Papers	Steering wheel	Purse
Door frame	Furniture	Door handle
Weapon	Window ledge	Sleeping bag
Blanket	Purse	Mitten
Cup or glass		

Use a sterile collection gauze pad to collect scent from a knife.
Photo by Jan Tweedie

Using a weapon (gun) for a scent article can be very tricky. The scent collection area is located on the trigger, trigger guard and the grips of the weapon. Use a pencil, pen, stick or wooden spoon handle to insert in the barrel of the weapon to lift the weapon off the ground, and collect the scent from both sides of the grips. Stay away from gunpowder residue, and *never* use the barrel of a recently fired gun or empty casings as scent collection sites. The overpowering smell of gunpowder will ruin or distort the scent and render the item useless for working the dog. You can also ruin critical evidence by swabbing the weapon.

To pick up an article of clothing or other portable scent article invert a plastic bag over your hand and grab the item, pulling backwards and into the bag without touching the article itself.

Commonly Used Scent Article Containers

Paper bag	Plastic bag	Un-deodorized trash bag
Styrofoam cup	Lunch sack	Evidence bag
Seal-A-Meal bag envelope		

Sealing a scent article as evidence means following a prescribed handling method called the "chain of evidence" to preserve evidence. The person who isolates the scent article (first handles it) must seal the item and place his or her initials or signature across the seal. The date and time the article became evidence should be included on the article bag as well as the location from which it was obtained. Every time the article changes hands the person receiving the article must indicate the time and date of change as well as the reason the article was transferred from the previous custodian. Again, the article label must be signed.

The key to selecting a scent article is to choose that article which has the least chance of being contaminated and is most saturated with the scent of the missing person. It is also important that the scent article be packaged by the handler or secured to decrease the chance of contamination.

If someone other than the handler will be collecting the scent article, it is imperative that the utmost caution be taken to avoid contamination. Instruct the person who will be collecting the item as to what type of article you want and how to collect it.

Commonly Used Scent Article Collection Tools

Coat hanger	Ruler	Pencil
Pliers	Wrench	Wooden spoon
Inverted bag	Stick	Gauze pad
Crowbar	Knife	Pen
Crutch	Baton	Tire iron

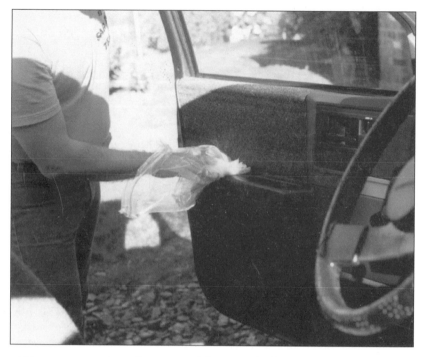

When someone has disappeared from a vehicle and there is no easily collected scent article, one can be made by using a gauze pad on the arm rest, steering wheel or head rest. PHOTO BY JAN TWEEDIE

Give the person two or three of your article bags and instruct the person to use a coat hanger, wooden spoon or broomstick to hold the item. Make sure the person understands that he or she must not lean on or stand over the item during the collection. To make sure that the chance of contamination is minimal, have the person who collects the article at the scene when you start your dog in case he or she must be eliminated by the dog.

There are several ways for a scent article to become contaminated. The item can be touched, bagged in a deodorized garbage bag (which promptly destroys the scent), inadvertently left open to the air if the seal is not closed, or transported improperly. Close and seal the bag and transport it in the trunk of the car out of the direct airflow and in a cool, dry area.

Guidelines for Gathering Scent Articles

To gather clothing scent articles:

1. Determine the best article of clothing for a scent article.
2. Choose a tool for picking up the item.
3. Determine the best container for the scent article.
4. Open the container carefully without leaning over it.
5. Place the container next to the chosen scent article.
6. Using the collection tool, pick up the item.
7. Place it in the container.
8. Close the container and seal.

To use a sterile collection kit:

1. Open one of the plastic bags without touching the inside.
2. Tear open one of the gauze pads without touching the pad.
3. Open the distilled water.
4. *Dampen* the gauze pad with the distilled water.
5. Invert the plastic bag over your hand.
6. Pick up the gauze pad with the inverted bag.
7. Squeeze off the excess water with clamps.
8. Wipe the gauze pad over the collection point.
9. Pull the pad into the bag without touching the pad.
10. Close and seal the bag.

Using the same scent article for more than one dog has varied results. Sometimes it has contaminated the article, but in other cases we have successfully scented several dogs from the same article. Try to make sure that your scent article is used only by your dog, and then secure it or take it with you on the trail.

If the scent article is to be retained by the investigating agency, the handler must provide a written description of the article with specific instructions as to how the article must be stored and maintained for your later use. Include instructions to keep the article frozen as well as a warning that exposure to air and the elements will significantly change the article's scent integrity.

Even a footprint can serve as a scent article. PHOTO BY JAN TWEEDIE

Use a tape recorder or a memo pad to write down the date, time and location of where a scent article was obtained as well as the case number and the type of crime. Make sure you log your collections. They will be needed for your mission report and may be very important in the criminal case that follows.

Always advise the law enforcement officer at the scene, the SAR coordinator, or the family as to what item(s) you have removed and be sure to return them following the conclusion of your work. In a criminal case it is permissible to retain the scent article as evidence in the event that it will be needed later in the case or during the trial.

The only reasons a scent article should be retained are in the cases of a criminal search where a line-up identification by the dog may be needed or if the lost person or the suspect were not located and you may be asked to search again. All other scent articles should be returned to the rightful owner or the investigating agency at the conclusion of your search.

Use your scent collection kit rather than removing a valuable piece of evidence. Always clear your presence and your activities with the officer in charge of the scene. To collect scent from a victim's clothing in the search for a suspect, be sure that the victim is available so the dog can eliminate that scent, and proceed with the search for the missing suspect. This is so the dog doesn't waste valuable time looking for the victim. The victim's scent will be more intense than the suspect's scent.

I have used a wide variety of scent articles, such as a footprint, window ledge, knife handle, purse, coffee cup, sheets, pillowcases, car seats, and steering wheels, with some being clearly better than others. In some searches, shoes, wallets, slippers, shirts, pants, and packs were used. Currency, a handkerchief, gun grips, rifle stocks, caps, sleeping bags, door handles, blankets, saddles, a suitcase or briefcase have been packaged. I have seen chairs, couches and magazines used for collecting scent lead to the missing person.

There have been times that we have been given scent articles that we thought were collected properly. The scent article was later determined to have been contaminated over and over, thrown in the back seat of someone's patrol car, never worn or recently laundered, or didn't belong to the missing person at all. When collecting a scent article make sure you know as much as you can about the article you are collecting.

SCENTING YOUR DOG

The best way to retain a scent article is to place it in a cool, dry place or freeze it. I freeze criminal scent articles as well as regular scent articles to protect the intensity of the scent in case the articles are used again. I use a tennis ball or film canister to hold the scent article I use for cadaver, arson, or blood searches. I take a new tennis ball, soak it in baking soda and water to remove the rubber smell and then air dry it outside. Once it is dry I cut a hole in the tennis ball, place the scent inside and then store the tennis ball in a *Ziploc* bag in the freezer. I use the same technique with the plastic film canister except that I keep two lids for each canister. I punch some small holes in one lid and leave the other lid intact. When the item is in the *Ziploc* bag in the freezer the solid lid is on. During thawing and use, the lid with the holes allows the scent to dissipate.

In harness and ready to go on the trail.
PHOTO BY ROBERT PEARCY.

When you scent the dog it is not necessary to pull the bag over his head or to force the dog's nose into the article. Scent the dog in a quiet place, away from distraction, at the point last seen. The dog may briefly consider the article and then begin working while other dogs will spend more time with the article, mouthing it or carrying it. Don't re-introduce the scent article over and over again just because you don't think the dog got a good enough whiff. Give the search command and get to work. If at all possible I take the scent article with me on the trail which allows me to re-scent the dog if we reach physical barrier that requires us to temporarily leave the trail or if we take a break on the trail for more than ten minutes. Digger liked to swim on breaks where water was available and would either continue the trail or wait in front of me to be re-scented. If he waited, I brought out the article, offered it to him, and off we went again.

Learning to trust your dog to follow a path of scent that we can neither see nor smell is the one of most difficult tasks of the search dog handler. Make sure your dog has the best possible chance of making a find by ensuring that your scent article is as good as possible.

Jonelle and Deputy Justin Smith, Larimer County, Colorado
Photo by Kent and Donna Dannen

"Waiting in the Wings"
ILLUSTRATION BY CRYSTAL MELVIN

CHAPTER SIX

Advanced Training

OBSTACLE TRAINING

The best trailing conditions are in effect on a moderate day (between forty-five and sixty-five degrees), over moist ground, with a slight (five-mile per hour) breeze and no falling precipitation. The best trailing terrain is level and basically flat and open with only light ground cover to hold the scent. It is unlikely that you will encounter all of these conditions on one trail. Training, therefore, must encompass varied types of terrain, weather conditions, and obstacles in order to prepare you for what will actually happen in the field. A trained search and rescue team should be able to search in any weather, in almost any terrain, and deal with unusual physical obstacles.

The first step is to get both the handler and the dog used to working in daylight and darkness, in dry conditions and in pouring rain. Remember, practice easy trails whenever you change the terrain or weather variables. After the dog has done well (run ten trails successfully), change one of the variables, such as working a night trail. As the dog masters this kind of trailing, add another variable.

TERRAIN

Beginner trails should be laid in fairly flat terrain with some vegetation. Totally open country is more difficult to work since vegetation acts to catch and hold scent. The terrain should be flat and the trail should be run in basically a straight line with no turns.

Once the dog works well and is successful on the simpler trails, it is time to change the scenery. Lay trails in unfamiliar terrain which has at least two terrain changes such as a hill, a small creek, or an intersecting road. Continue to change the terrain variables as the dog masters each task. Avoid changing things too quickly or adding more than one or two changes in a particular trail. Don't frustrate the dog and work slowly and carefully.

As you gain confidence in varied terrain, change the elements of the trail. Include trailing over gravel or pavement, through populated neighborhoods, across playgrounds saturated with scent, in shopping malls, parking lots, and buildings. Add various footings for the dog, such as creek crossings, bridges, asphalt, concrete and mud.

Remember to run fresh trails once in a while to keep the dog enthusiastic. Most trails on actual calls will be less than twenty-four hours old. A short, fresh trail will provide a break from new obstacles and allow the dog to do something he knows well—a good way to build success into your training!

BUILDING SEARCHES

Teaching the dog to work inside a building, on slippery floors, or in other enclosed structures is crucial for those handlers who want to work crime scenes or disaster scenes.

Start the dog on a simple, fresh trail such as a hide-and-seek or chase trail inside a building. This allows the dog to concentrate on the fresh scent. Walk the dog through the building before laying the trail, then have the runner lay the trail and proceed with the dog. One major concern for dogs is the footing. Be alert to the fact that linoleum and polished floors provide no traction for dogs. You will need to work the dog slowly enough to avoid slips or falls. Some handlers apply a spray-on product to the dog's paws to increase traction. However, this tacky substance contains chemicals which can easily mask the scent the dog is following.

Walk the dog over slippery surfaces as often as possible. Allow the dog to choose the best path—don't drag him. Forcing the dog to cross a foreign or slippery surface may cause the dog to panic and slip, possibly causing injury or frightening the dog. Some handlers place sawdust or a similar product on a slippery surface for practice. As the dog gains confidence the handler gradually removes the traction dust until the dog can cross slowly but confidently.

STAIRS AND LADDERS

Steps are another obstacle that must be overcome. Dogs are wary of stairs because they are unsure as to where to put their back feet.

Start training the dog on a closed stairway with steps that the dog cannot see through since seeing through the stairs will cause a dog to doubt the integrity of the footing. When this occurs, slow down and let the dog to choose the best path. Allow the dog to master this before moving on to an open stairwell.

Another method used to instill confidence on stairs involves two people. Attach a lead that is long enough to reach from the dog to where you, the handler, will be standing at the top of a short flight (less than ten steps) of stairs. Have the assisting person hold the dog at the base of the stairs while you climb to the top. Once you have reached the top of the stairs, call the dog and have a treat ready. The dog will usually whine and move back and forth at the bottom of the staircase.

If the dog refuses to go up the stairs, call the dog and tug on the lead. If the dog still continues to balk, move halfway down the steps and again call the dog and tug on the lead. Do not ever drag a dog up the stairs!

Another method is to place the dog halfway up the stairs and then go forward, allowing the dog no way out other than to climb or descend. Encouragement will ensure a positive response. It will take more than one effort to accomplish this, but be patient.

Open stairway training should follow the same procedure. It may take the dog longer to build confidence, but starting a puppy early on stair climbing will minimize the fear.

A dog can learn to climb and descend a ladder although the heavier breeds may experience some difficulty in maintaining balance and may try to jump from the top instead of climbing down. Ladders are used to teach a dog to pay attention to footing. Start with the ladder flat on the ground and allow the dog to become familiar with moving through the rungs. Elevate the ladder slightly, four to six inches, and again let the dog get used to moving from rung to rung. Gradually increase the height of the ladder to a maximum of ten inches off the ground. This kind of training helps the dog to learn how to place his feet when moving through debris at a disaster site.

ELEVATORS

Elevators are encountered in most multi-story complexes. The closed doors and strange movement of the elevator will distress many dogs until they are familiar with them. Some dogs experience a claustrophobic reaction when the elevator door closes. Practice using elevators often, acclimating the dog to the smells, sounds and vibrations.

Enter the elevator and step to the rear of the car and practice entering and exiting the elevator without going up or down. Once the dog gets used to walking into this tiny room, walk in and push the buttons to go up one floor. Before the elevator moves, you must reassure the dog and telegraph confidence. Once the dog is comfortable going up several floors, practice going down. Have someone waiting outside the door with a treat or lots of attention to make the trip a positive experience for the dog.

WATER CROSSINGS

You will eventually encounter water if you spend any time at all searching outside. Teaching the dog to work a scent that parallels water, crosses a bridge or goes through the water takes practice!

Training a dog to work around water crossings begins simply by finding a small creek that you can easily step across. Have your runner lay a fresh trail that crosses the creek and command the dog to follow the trail. If the dog stops at the water, urge him across to pick up the scent on the other side. As the dog's ability increases, so should the distance across the creek until the dog can cross a six- to eight-foot-wide creek and pick up the trail on the other side.

Once the dog is comfortable with this, have the runner go up- or downstream and emerge above or below the entrance point. The runner can also walk up the creek as part of the trail. The dog may work the bank or the water. The dog will probably work the water if the runner is upstream since scent will float on the water and is easily followed. Using flagged trails for this training will help the handler reinforce positive work. Remember that flagged trails should be used only occasionally.

AERIAL CROSSINGS

Familiarize the dog with heights and with crossing bridges. Train using all kinds of bridges, including those you dislike. Teach the dog to walk across a wide tree crossing a stream, starting small and close to the ground at first and build until you are both confident enough to handle the higher crossings. Often a dog's reluctance to cross is because he can see the moving water or he perceives that the surface is not strong enough to support him. Include piers, trestles, docks, platforms, scaffolds, and other types of crossings. Encourage the dog up and across while keeping him under control. Practice this as often as possible.

CULVERTS AND TUNNELS

Culverts present another interesting obstacle for a dog. Since they resemble a tunnel but have strange footing (ribbed bottoms in some cases), the dog may balk at first. The handler should leave the dog at one end and call the dog from the other end of the culvert. This will usually be all that is necessary to get the dog to move through.

I asked permission to train my dogs in the Public Works storage yard. It is full of big culvert pipes, boards, culvert grates and piles of gravel. It contains lots of things to climb through and around and I don't have to worry about water flowing through the pipes in the practice area.

Be careful in the field when using culverts that drain excess water, especially during flood seasons and during or after a rain storm, as dangerous levels of water can rise without warning. Most playgrounds have large culverts as part of the play equipment and utilizing these above-ground pipes is a safe training alternative.

We also infrequently train in mine shafts and caves. These areas are *extremely* dangerous. Be sure that you have an experienced Mine Rescue Team training with you to familiarize you with mine search techniques. Never train or practice in these areas alone. This kind of searching requires specialized equipment, including headlamps, helmets, gloves, protective clothing, maps and a clear understanding of mine gases and other related hazards. If the hounds lead me to a mine shaft I always pass the continuance of the trail to the experienced Mine Rescue Team.

GAME AND OTHER ANIMALS

Wild animals are often encountered on wilderness searches. A search dog that wanders off to chase animals or follow game trails is not reliable and so it is vital that you teach the dog not to alert or to respond to them. By using the "Out!" command followed by a strong tug on the lead, the dog should return to working the trail. Do not allow the dog to stop and investigate animal droppings. The dog should not be frightened of game but will be naturally curious. Work the dog often in areas populated by groups of wild game and small animals to get him used to the different smells and sounds.

We lived on an eighty-acre game farm when Digger was a puppy. He became so used to the fawns and other wild animals that were dropped off for rehabilitation or returned to the woods that he would just ignore them. Ben and Kady were fascinated by cows and other domestic animals and so we incorporated the animals into the training sessions. Over time both dogs learned to ignore them as well as the wild game.

I recommend that search dogs not be used to look for lost animals if their main role is intended to searching for humans. It is very difficult breaking the habit of trailing animals.

JUMPS

Teaching your dog to jump over obstacles in his path on command will condition a dog to continue working a trail containing downed timber, boards or debris across the path as well as save your back a lot of agony. Start by setting up some small jumps using a broomstick or a piece of wood across two concrete blocks.

Lead the dog up to the jump and give him the "Over!" command while pulling forward on the lead. Make sure that he can see over and beyond the jump. If he can't he may balk. I often start the dogs jumping things as we play in the yard when the dog is off-lead.

Start out with the jump very close to the ground, and as you raise the level of the jump, give the command farther away from the obstacle to allow the dog enough speed and forward motion to clear the jump. Work slowly until the dog clears a jump that is twenty-four inches high and at least ten inches wide. Dragging a dog over a jump by the choke chain will not encourage the dog to think independently. Instead it will cause the dog to associate the jump with trauma.

I *discourage* my dogs from jumping fences. I do not want to teach my dogs that it is acceptable to jump a fence of restraining height. In fact, I rarely will use fencing material as a jumping prop. I expect my hounds to respect a fence and require my assistance in dealing with it as opposed to treating it like another fun thing to jump. I teach them the "Wait!" command and walk them around the fence or to a gate.

One handler I know taught his dog Crescent to jump fences that were set up in the obstacle course. The fences were the same kind of mesh he had used in Crescent's kennel. Marc taught Crescent that if he could not jump the fence outright he could climb up and over, using the mesh as footholds. Crescent was a terrific climber, able to cross all the barriers in any obstacle course. Not surprisingly he was also able to climb his kennel and yard fences. Marc called for help after Crescent narrowly escaped being hit by a car after he let himself out. I suggested that a cover be firmly attached to the top of Crescent's run to prevent such escapes. Marc's second dog, Knight, was not trained to jump or climb fences but instead he waits patiently to be escorted around or lifted over the barrier.

NOISE

Noise is an obstacle that can be one of the most difficult to overcome. It is well known that dogs don't forget frightening experiences or noises, so expose the dog to as many different noises as possible while the dog is young. Lawn mowers, radios, traffic, horns, gunfire, and fireworks are some of the most frightening noises for the dogs. I keep a radio programmed to a station that has a variety of programs with the dogs at all times.

Keep in mind that dogs have very sensitive hearing. Your goal is to try to desensitize the dog, not deafen it. Keep volumes turned down to avoid blaring but loud enough for the dog to hear. I turn the volume up during thunder storms since the dogs prefer music to thunder.

To accustom the dog to gunfire, it is best to enlist the help of a professional, preferably a reputable person who trains hunting dogs. Approach this training very slowly. Start with a BB or pellet gun and have an assistant fire the weapon while you stand next to and reassure the dog. Always start with your assistant at least one hundred yards or more from the dog, and move no closer than five yards away from the dog. Lots of praise and patting will make the experience easier for the dog. As the dog learns to ignore the report of the weapon, increase the caliber.

Gunfire makes my ears hurt and I wear headphones on the shooting range to protect my hearing. I also believe in protecting the dogs' hearing and will put headphones on them to muffle the sounds as much as possible. Gradually you can expose them to louder sounds.

Fireworks terrorize dogs every year. Digger and Angel were deathly afraid of fireworks and went right through a cedar fence late one night to escape the noise. Starting early in the dog's life it's best to accustom the dog to gunfire and fireworks and to teach them that you are their safety net, to run to you for comfort and protection. Some dogs will never get over their fear of the report. This does not disqualify the dog from search work, but the handler must be aware of the fear and be prepared for the response.

Expose your puppy or dog to traffic noises including quickly accelerating vehicles, skidding tires, honking horns and screeching brakes; the sound of air brakes can be very intimidating to the dog. Walk the dog down city streets to familiarize him with the variety and volume of sounds in a city environment. Provide a lot of practice and patience. Work trails along busy streets to focus the dog's attention on working and you will be rewarded with a dog that performs well under stress.

STRAY ANIMALS

Wandering dogs and cats can easily distract your working dog so it is best to avoid them. When on a search in a residential area, it is imperative that you watch for loose dogs and keep them away from your dog because they will view your restrained dog as an easy mark. I often carry a few rocks with me and when I encounter a loose dog I rein my dog in close, swing the end of the lead, yell and pitch the rocks. Or, if I am working with a backup handler, they can spook the loose dog away and keep watch for others. An aggressive dog may take more force but when you are working criminal searches you can ask the accompanying officer to watch for and get rid of stray animals on the trail.

WORKING AROUND HELICOPTERS

On many searches the dog teams are transported to a search area by helicopter. The noise and vibration of a helicopter can be distressing for anyone, especially a dog.

To help a dog familiarize himself to the sight and smell of a helicopter, begin with the helicopter turned off and empty. With the doors open so that the dog can see inside, walk the dog around and alongside the machine. Encourage the dog to take a look inside and lift the dog into the passenger area of the helicopter, climbing in with him. Take a seat and encourage the dog to lie down or sit beside you. This may take some time.

The next hurdle is a helicopter in motion. Have the pilot start the helicopter and using a short lead walk the dog towards the chopper, confidently but slowly. Plenty of reassurance will be necessary. Once you get to the open doors, get some assistance loading the dog into the cockpit. Take a seat and have the dog sit or lie down next to you. Do not allow the dog to stand or walk around.

Almost all dogs will shy away from the noise and vibration of a helicopter. Use calm reassurance. The next step in helicopter training is to actually take a flight. Use the same calm helicopter approach and loading process. Take a seat, reassuring the dog constantly if needed. There is no room in a helicopter for a frantic or fighting dog, so it is critical that you maintain tight control over your dog. Some dogs may require a muzzle prior to flying in a helicopter while others must be crated. A dog that requires such safeguards will not frequently be used for searches that require helicopter transport.

DISASTER TRAINING

Search and rescue dog teams respond to natural disasters all over the world. They can involve a variety of terrain, both stable and unstable, being in the field for long periods of work, and a variety of weather conditions. Disaster work means primitive living facilities, travel, and exposure to death and destruction on a large scale. Floods, tornadoes, collapsed buildings, mud slides and earthquakes have all been worked by experienced dog teams, saving numerous lives in the midst of total chaos.

Following the Mexico City earthquakes in 1985, several American dog teams responded to assist in locating victims buried in the rubble of the city. Handlers recovered many bodies and spent numerous hours in the field. News footage covering the event portrays workers with eyes reflecting total fatigue and shock. Disaster work is emotionally draining and extremely stressful.

Handler safety is one of the key issues in disaster searching and many people believe that dogs should be worked off-lead to reduce the occurrence of handlers following dogs into dangerous buildings among falling or loose debris from a collapsed structure. This sentiment is felt so strongly by some people that they believe that if the dog cannot be worked off-lead, then the dog should not work in disaster situations.

Another school of thought encourages the handler and the dog to make the safety determination themselves. In many cases a handler may choose to work the dog on a much longer lead (up to fifty feet) to give the dog more mobility. In most disaster areas, there are human rescuers that work alongside the dog teams to recover victims or investigate alerts. Handlers that support on-lead searches believe that if an area is so fragile that a human being would break through the debris, then it is an unnecessary risk even for a dog to take. Even if a victim was found by a dog, a person would not be able to access and rescue the victim.

Unfortunately, harness and on-lead dogs are frequently overlooked. During several international disasters, dogs from the United States responded to assist in the recovery of victims but only off-lead dogs were allowed to respond. Tethered dogs were not invited and consequently have been discouraged from working disaster scenes.

While there are definite advantages to having an off-lead dog in a disaster situation, there is a place for on-lead dogs as well. In many instances the teams could work together with on-lead dogs working more stable buildings and rubble piles indicating areas of potential interest. These areas can then be followed up by an off-lead dog team. Tunnels and collapsed buildings can also be checked by off-lead search dogs. Ideally, the ability of the search dog, not the limitations of the equipment, should be the deciding factor.

The other thing that cannot be overlooked involves team-work. The on-lead dog handlers may be the best people to provide overhead and support for the off-lead teams. These support members locate food, water, shelter and supplies, brief and debrief the searchers, map areas covered and generally take care of all of the details related to getting and keeping dogs in the field. It is an excellent opportunity for teams to learn one another's skills and abilities and it frees up other off-lead team members to work while the support teams take care of the other business.

Disaster work often involves recovering bodies from unstable buildings. After repeated exposure to cadavers, many dogs will lose interest in continuing the search. Handlers on the scene of a disaster can work together to play hide and seek to give the dogs the opportunity and the positive reinforcement of locating a live person. This is done to boost the dogs' emotional stamina to enable them to continue the search.

Disaster work demands that the handler and the dog be in excellent physical condition. The team must be ready to respond quickly to any place on the globe so be prepared with a valid passport, current vaccinations for the dog, and a health certificate.

TRAINING FOR DISASTER SEARCHES

Disaster training requires dedication and consistency. The toughest part of the training is locating an appropriate training area which will simulate the rubble or debris of a disaster site. A training area can be specifically constructed to include obstacles that may be encountered in the field, such as culverts, loose rock, water, ladders, narrow, elevated walkways and jumps. Teams have also used abandoned buildings and the rubble at the site of a demolished building. Be sure to get permission from the owner before using these areas, since the owner's liability is extremely high in such hazardous sites. Expect resistance.

The handler must have and use basic safety equipment. Heavy gloves, a helmet or hard hat, a headlamp, protective work boots, and protective outer clothing are required for all workers. Ropes and climbing equipment can also come in handy. A filter mask is useful for working in dust, dirt or around cadavers.

Just as in basic training, it is important to expose the dog to a wide variety of environments to prepare for the realities of the field. But remember, confusing the dog with too much stimuli will lead to problems in the field.

The first step is acclimating the dog to a wide variety of surfaces to increase the dog's confidence and agility. Begin with a rocky road or gravel area to familiarize the dog with working in and along a roadway. Increase the difficulty by working slippery surfaces like muddy or flooded areas and loose rock. River or creek banks and ground covered by wood, loose dirt and other debris prepare the dog for working in rubble.

To improve a dog's balance, place a board (at least twenty inches wide) across concrete blocks to create an elevated walkway, making sure that the walkway is long enough to prevent the dog from jumping from one end to the other. Start

Larry Allen taught Jethro to rappel down hillsides. Here Larry and Jethro get ready for another trip down the hill.
PHOTO BY JAN TWEEDIE

with the board very low to the ground, increasing the height as the dog gains confidence. Next place the board at an angle and walk the dog up and down the angled plank. Start with a slight angle and slowly increase it. The beam, or elevated walkway, will prepare the dog for working in elevated rubble areas.

Ladders, window jumps and hurdles are helpful in establishing balance and movements used in disaster work. Culverts will teach the dog to move through a tunnel or narrow opening. *Do not use* service outlets or manholes. These can be dangerous and may not have an alternative exit in case of an emergency. Playgrounds are excellent training areas since many have large pieces of equipment. Slides, piers or walkways, nets for climbing, loose, sandy ground cover and climbing equipment are built-in and accessible. I will also train puppies to go down a slide by going with them. A slide is a situation where the dog cannot control his descent. In disaster work or loose rubble situations the dog may have to slide with a moving piece of debris. The dog learns to use the motion of the slide to stay on top of debris and can jump to safety when possible.

Other good places that usually require that you obtain permission are lumber yards, telephone or public works storage yards and storage lots. Be careful around gravel quarries because they often contain holes and shifting dirt or gravel which can bury you quickly and without warning. Building supply yards with stacks of lumber and pipes are dangerous places to train unless you are very careful. Be sure to get permission before using private property.

Your dog's safety is the most critical issue during obstacle training. If the dog suffers a fall or becomes scared, the handler must provide reassurance and encourage the dog to try the exercise again to rebuild confidence. One bad experience can frighten the dog for life so work slowly to establish confidence.

Have a runner hide underneath some debris, scent the dog or command the dog to find, and allow the dog to work. Keep the dog working at a slow and steady pace to avoid slips and falls. When the dog alerts or indicates he has the find, the handler must be able to access the dog or direct responders to where the dog is. Praise will be the pay off the dog is looking for.

Training the dog to work in a disaster area is important for a number of reasons. In earthquakes, floods and mud slides the dog will work through water, mud and debris. The dog must be used to working a trail in those conditions. As ability increases, the variability of the obstacles encountered and the difficulty of trail terrain should increase.

Using sheets of plywood, clothing and cardboard boxes you can simulate a buried victim. Have the runner lay the trail and lie down at the end. Either the runner himself or a third person can cover the runner with the clothing or debris. You can also find or create a shallow depression in the ground, such as a trench, and lay the materials over it. Make sure that the runner has an emergency exit and that air circulation in the trench is clear and free of debris. Be sure that the runner is able to get out from under the makeshift debris with no assistance in case of an emergency.

Once the victim is in position, harness the dog and give the work command. The dog may initially shy away from the buried runner; if this happens the runner can call the dog. This kind of alert indicates the dog has found something but it is better for the dog to nose the debris, or bark and paw at the items covering the runner. Most dogs will rush up for the find but are unsure how to access the "victim" under the covering. If the dog is unable to find the runner, have the runner call for help periodically. This will help the dog focus his search and also exposes the dog to a sound he will hear in the field.

Stay close to the dog during the initial phases of training to watch for alerts. The dog may alert by barking, wagging his tail, digging or lying down. Your dog will choose its own method of telling you what's going on.

Once the dog finds the runner, remove the debris to allow the dog to complete the find. The runner should praise the dog enthusiastically but after the dog masters this phase, use a runner that remains silent throughout the exercise to simulate a cadaver search.

The items used to cover the runner should be varied, becoming increasingly more complicated. Instead of boards try using bricks or a light covering of dirt. *Never completely cover a runner with snow or dirt, which could lead to suffocation and death.* A trench covered with boards or drywall works fine. Remember that safety is always your first concern. If you want to work snow or avalanche situations, make sure that your runner is well insulated with a clear emergency escape.

Train for disaster work frequently. Make the work interesting by creating search problems ranging from a quick search and recovery to those situations requiring as long as two or three hours to solve. I recommend training with other teams to help the team develop skills and a strong partnership in distracting environments.

CADAVER TRAINING

Search dogs are used to find human remains in a variety of crime scenes. The age of the burial site, the conditions of the remains, the abilities of the dog and the desires of the handler will all directly influence whether the search dog will alert on a deceased human body.

Some handlers choose not to work in this type of search in which the images can become overwhelming. Handlers may be haunted by nightmares of the scene. In any case, the dog handler must decide whether or not the team will respond to body recoveries or crime scene searches *before* they are called out.

A dog may shy away from the smell of a deceased or decomposing human body; dogs may become depressed and refuse to make the find. The dog also may become protective of his handler or of the body. Training for recovering human remains is for the strong of service and strong of stomach.

For training purposes, trainers can use several different substances to simulate the smell of a decomposing body, including rotted pig's knuckles, rotted animal flesh and chemicals.

There are chemical companies that manufacture substances to mimic the scent of decaying flesh. Some people believe that the chemical works as effectively as actual cadaver remains and that it is much easier to get and much less messy. The Sigma Chemical Company located in St. Louis, Missouri manufactures two versions of this substance, Formulation 1 and 2. This company also manufactures other canine training aids, including pseudo-narcotics for training drug dogs. Remember that these pseudo-scents are toxic and must be handled with care and caution.

The main drawback to chemical scents is that they are packaged in single-use, glass ampoules. The ampoules have snap-off caps and, once opened, must be thrown away. The cost is about six dollars per ampoule.

The best thing to use for training is the real thing: decayed or decomposing human remains. Human remains are hard to come by and the possession of remains may be against the law in your state without a permit. Keep in mind that human remains will continue to decompose and are extremely aromatic unless they are frozen. It is best to freeze the remains and thaw them out for training or a search. Some handlers store the remains in a cool place, such as a garage, but I have found that the odor will penetrate almost any material and is

Digger indicating cadaver scent. PHOTO BY JAN TWEEDIE

very hard to eliminate. I do not recommend burying cadaver material between uses because dogs or other animals will dig it up, rolling in it, and may consume it.

Remains that have been treated with formaldehyde or embalming fluid cannot be used because the chemicals used in the embalming process render the item useless for training or scenting a dog. The chemicals prevent or alter the natural decomposition process which inhibits the remains from emitting the odor that the dog will detect on a search.

Once you have established a working relationship with local authorities, it may be easier to secure your training material. Some medical examiners or coroners will refuse to release remains. Other medical examiners may be willing to work through your emergency services director or a local physician.

Never handle human remains with your bare hands; use gloves and pliers or a similar tool. Handling rotting remains without gloves or tools can result in serious infections or illness if you come in contact with superficial cuts or abrasions or mucous membranes.

The scent article does not have to be large; in fact, most handlers that work with cadaver scent use very little of the remains. A small section of bone with the marrow intact is the best source of scent material. A piece of the rib or sternum and a little tissue will also serve as an adequate article.

Once you have the remains, put them in an airtight container such as a peanut butter jar which is a heavy plastic jar with a wide mouth. I prefer plastic containers because glass containers may break, creating quite a mess and possibly destroying your scent article. Whatever container you choose, be sure it is clean and odorless before use. This can be accomplished by washing the jar thoroughly, removing any label and the cardboard lid liner, and then running the jar through two dishwasher cycles.

If you are planning to use a plastic container make sure it has been deodorized using baking soda and water solution (mix one cup baking soda with water) to fill the container to the rim. Let the solution sit for twenty-four to forty-eight hours. Empty the jar and repeat if necessary.

Add a few drops of distilled water to your clean and odorless container and place the cadaver material in the jar. Put the lid on, and shake the container gently to coat the material with water drops to keep the article moist and provide a more realistic scent.

Store the cadaver material in the back of a freezer if possible, in the jar wrapped in opaque, clearly labeled plastic bags.

I advise handlers to gradually familiarize themselves with the smell so they will be able to identify it in the field. While holding your breath, open the container of thawed material and place it on the ground. Stand up and breathe. If you cannot detect a faint musty odor, lean forward a little at a time until you notice the smell.

Decaying human remains will continue to emit an odor as long as there is flesh attached to the bones or if there is bone marrow that has not dried up. Clothing that covered the cadaver will continue to emit the odor long after the flesh has decomposed. The odor of decaying remains may nauseate some handlers. This is perfectly normal. Remember, cadaver work is not for everyone.

Next, find out how the dog reacts to the material. Place the cadaver material, opened, on the ground. Harness or attach the working collar to your dog and place the dog on-lead. Walk over to the material and watch the dog. Most dogs are curious and will investigate the smell, although some dogs will shy abruptly away from it. Either alert is an excellent indicator for you in the field. Some dogs will excitedly approach the container and attempt to retrieve the material inside. While objectionable to humans, this is a natural behavior exhibited by all predators. Do not allow the dog, for any reason, to consume any part of the object. Try this exercise several times to make sure you understand the alert for cadaver material.

Establish a specific command for your dog to find cadaver material. The command should be different from any other start command. Many handlers have used "Dig!" while others use a name or variety of terms. Pick one command and stick with it. Every time you challenge the dog to find the cadaver material, give the same command. Praise the dog for the alert, and give your command for off-trail or quit. Secure the dog out of sight, and move the container. Repeat the process until the dog makes a find on the material every time.

Learn to read the dog's actions but be aware that some dogs will react to cadaver material in the field totally differently than they do in training. The dog may shy away from the smell, attempt to run, bark or cower. Other dogs will attempt to eat the remains. If you are not comfortable working with cadaver material, it is still a good idea to use it in training to learn what your dog will do when he finds it.

Once your dog's response is clear, take the container into the field and partially bury it in dirt or under leaves in a training area. Make sure you remember where the item is. The location can be marked with a section of grid tape placed out of sight of the dog.

Harness the dog and walk him, downwind, within ten yards of the container. Give the command you have chosen. When the dog alerts on the container or finds the container, praise him generously and after taking him off-lead, give him a treat.

If the dog does not locate the article or does not alert, move him within five yards of the container, and repeat the process. Continue to move the dog closer until the dog gives you the alert. Praise the dog for his work and again offer him a treat or toy.

If your dog shies away from the container to indicate his alert, work with the dog until you can figure out the direction the alert is indicating as well as the proximity of the item to the dog.

To increase the difficulty in this exercise, move the container, burying it, covering it with leaves, suspending it from a limb or overhang, or placing it under your vehicle. Repeat the exercise several times over a period of days until you are confident that the dog is making a clear find and that you can read what the dog is indicating.

As your dog masters various obstacles and training, try hiding the material in a box or bucket with a lid. Bury the item, place it in a barrel, a vehicle trunk, suitcase, or similar item and work the dog on this.

If your dog enjoys a tennis ball, consider placing a couple of balls in the container with your scent material. Then just throw the ball into the brush for the dog to find. Tennis balls are easier to bury and are less trouble to replace than the actual cadaver material and a tennis ball will quickly absorb the scent of the cadaver material.

Searching for cadaver material in the field requires a great deal of training. First, using the scent article, or the ball, plant the article and allow at least fifteen minutes to pass before you command the dog to find it. Roll the ball through brush to teach the dog to follow the cadaver trail to the primary site. Gradually allow more time to pass before sending the dog and watch him closely; the age of the remains on a search will often determine the strength of the alert. Once the dog is able to find the article that has been out for more than one hour, slowly increase the starting distance.

Never increase two difficulty factors at once. Increase the time *or* the distance, not both. Make sure that you end each work session with a success. If this means doing an elementary trail or search, so be it.

Terrain, weather and ground conditions will have an effect on the dog's success rate. Challenging terrain includes rocks, hills, drainages and clearings. Make sure that you include a variety of these terrain components during training.

Weather conditions like precipitation and wind can also pose problems for cadaver recovery teams. Whenever possible, work the dog into the wind during cadaver searches to give the dog the greatest access to the cadaver scent. Mild precipitation increases the scent of the cadaver but heavy rains can wash the drifted scent off the foliage and ground cover. Practice in the rain whenever possible. Snow will preserve scent in the primary site but the outside temperature may limit the drifting scent. Ground conditions will also greatly affect the scent. Frozen ground gives off little scent; very dry and dusty ground does not hold scent well either.

The first body that Digger recovered will stick in my mind forever. Digger was about fifteen months old when we were called to search for a sixty-two year old local man who had not returned from a rock hunting trip. The call came around midnight when the man's truck was found parked along a deserted stretch of highway. I harnessed Digger, Angel and Jethro and scented them from a down vest in the front seat of the truck.

While the SAR Coordinator was sending the ground searchers across the road and to the east, the hounds took off to the west. Within one-half mile, all three dogs were pulling hard straining forward to tag the man lying still on the ground.

Digger began whining and leaned into me, refusing to move. He was trembling and baying. Angel was lying quietly with her head on her paws and Jethro just stood there with his head down and his tail between his legs.

While we waited for the ground team to arrive to carry the body out, Digger became very protective of me and warned the other dogs to stay back. He whined and paced and tried pulling me away from the body, clearly trying to separate me from the dead man. We had to wait for a while before the body could be removed.

For the next three days Digger whined and cried whenever I left. It had been a traumatic experience for him. He was not afraid of the body; in fact, he tried to mark it, but it was as though he wasn't going to let the same thing happen to me. On every body recovery afterward, Digger appeared depressed following the search.

After any practice or actual search for a cadaver or cadaver material I strongly advise that you set up a live-find scenario with a happy ending for the dog. This reminds him that death is not the result of every search. Following a search I will often take Ben to a school or nursing home or someplace where he will get lots of love and attention. It seems to help him bounce back after recovering a body.

The important thing to remember about cadaver searches is that your reaction to the first recovery will determine how and if you will respond again. If you find a deceased person it is natural to be curious and saddened, and, depending on the condition of the remains, you may become ill. Even the most seasoned veteran will react to a body in bad condition. Talk to other handlers about how they felt when they recovered their first body and talk to handlers about how you feel. One of the best ways to deal with anxiety and fear is to talk it through with someone who has had the same or a similar experience. Don't be afraid or embarrassed to show how you feel. Post-traumatic stress is common.

Spend extra time with your dog following a recovery and work on other kinds of training for the next few days. Your feelings and how you deal with the mission will be telegraphed to your dog so you may choose to take a break for a day or so, but get back into the training routine quickly.

If you are used in a criminal search, you will be expected to write a detailed report and provide written documentation of your training records and qualifications. Make sure that you have a written record of every training session involving cadaver material.

SEARCHING A FIRE SCENE

Arson and natural disaster fires are also scenarios in which search dogs are used to detect human remains. A scent article that has been charred is hard to work with because the burned smell easily overpowers the original scent. Fire victims are often unrecognizable and a dog working a fire scene for human remains is not searching for the original scent of the missing person. Fire scene searching is much like cadaver searching in that respect.

Before you start training for fire scene work, choose a new command and get the necessary equipment for both the handler and the dog. Equipment must be durable and washable. After working a fire scene the equipment will be laden with the charred smell of the fire; washing the equipment will usually get rid of the odors and keep the equipment in better shape. Oil of peppermint or wintergreen can be applied to the filter mask to cover the odor of the charred remains.

The scent article used for fire scene training, and to start the dog at an actual scene, is charred cadaver material. Most handlers have a limited amount of cadaver material to begin with and are reluctant to use it for fire scene training since the remains must be scorched to the first degree or charred as the dog advances in training. Some handlers that do not have access to cadaver material have had some success with using burned, spoiled pig knuckles, but the best scent article is the real thing, unpleasant as it is.

The key to using a scent article with such an overpowering odor is limiting the dog's exposure, allowing the dog only a slight whiff of the material. Divide your scent material into two parts. One part you will save for future use. The second part of the scent material will be used for training. Char part of the training material and then divide this material into two sections, one section being larger than the other.

Equipment List

1 working collar
1 18" traffic lead
1 6' standard lead
1 10' working lead
5 filter masks
1 container w/lid
1 container with holes in lid
1 pair heavy gloves
6 pair disposable rubber gloves
1 flashlight
1 small bottle peppermint or wintergreen oil

Place the larger section of the scent material in a container with a lid, punching holes in the lid to allow the scent to escape. Hide the burned cadaver material in the open at the outer fringe of the fire scene. This will be the quarry that the dog is seeking. Place the remaining scent material in a second container. This container should have a lid with no holes in it. This is the scent article for working the fire scene. Once the quarry container is in position, harness the dog and expose the dog to the scent material giving the dog the working command.

The beginning fire scene dog will alert on anything charred until the quarry is located. Let the dog work the trail out. As the dog works, use plenty of praise. Move the quarry farther into the fire scene as the dog is able to locate it. Once the dog is clearly identifying the remains, cover them with burned wood or cardboard, and advance to partially burying the remains as the dog's skill increases.

As a final test, cover the quarry with charred debris. The most advanced level of fire victim recovery is when a dog can locate and uncover buried cadaver material in a fire pit. Training the dog to locate victims that have been soaked with fuel is another challenge. Handlers can use scent articles that have been slightly contaminated with gasoline, but it is common for the material to be overpowered by the smell of the petroleum product. Start with a slight contamination and increase the level of contamination as the dog progresses.

Fire scene training is difficult and takes more time than other types of search training. However, once the dog is able to differentiate the human scent from the strong char smell the training moves more quickly.

WATER SEARCHING

You should work on water problems only if you want to be called on drownings, boating accidents and other related missions. You will need a personal flotation device (a vest-style life jacket) and strong swimming skills in the event the dog plunges into the water, taking you with him. Water search problems are particularly tough for the dog that does not like water so you can save yourself a lot of time and trouble by knowing in advance whether your dog will take to water or not.

I encourage my dogs to swim and play in the water. Not only is it a great way to cool off in the hot summer it is also a fun way to introduce a dog to water searching.

For training purposes, you will need a runner that is SCUBA certified. To start the exercise, have a runner lay a short trail that enters a creek or pond. The runner should move out of sight but remain in the water. Allow the dog to work the trail. If the dog stops or balks at the water, encourage the dog to continue to make the find.

Next, have the diver lay a trail into the water, submerging fairly close to the surface and within twenty feet of the water's edge. Once the diver is in place, command the dog to work. When the dog reaches the water, encourage him to go in for the find. If the dog balks or refuses to enter the water, don't feel too discouraged; remember that this is an alert indicating that the runner is in the water. Water alerts may be different from land alerts, so pay attention to the dog's body language. Have the diver surface and swim closer to shore to be found. Repeat the exercise until the dog either enters the water or else you are very familiar with the alert which indicates that the runner is in or under the water.

As the dog becomes more adept in the water, the next step is to age the trail and for the diver to go further beneath the surface, despite the fact that most drowning victims will surface after a while, depending on the water and air temperatures. Next have the diver move off shore farther to make it necessary for the dog to swim out a short distance. Then move the trail off the edge of a dock or pier. Watch how the dog alerts.

Getting the dog used to riding in a boat is your next challenge. Start out with a rowboat or small boat on dry ground. Once the dog has mastered getting in and out, put the boat in shallow water and have the dog get in and out of the boat. The dog may become afraid if the boat starts rocking back and forth, so have someone steady it. Once the dog will get in and sit or lie down, slowly take the boat out onto the water. Stay close to shore until you are sure the dog won't leap out of the boat. When the dog is comfortable in a rowboat switch to a motorboat, using the same slow progression to instill confidence in the dog. Jet boats make a lot of noise and may take additional time for the dog to become accustomed to them.

Put the dog in the boat and have him work the scent floating on the water to determine where the diver is. You may want the diver to use a small float or tape to mark where they are so you can watch for the dog's alert. Gradually the flagged trails should be stopped and the dog's alerts should be the sole tip-off to the diver's location.

You will need to work in a variety of weather and wind conditions to build a reliable water search team. You may also want the diver to take along a container of cadaver scent and to release a small amount of the scent underwater for water cadaver searches.

A search dog will work the water from either the bow or the side of the boat while the boat driver maneuvers the boat as the dog indicates. Some dogs will leap overboard when they have located the missing person so be prepared to restrain your dog if necessary; some handlers keep the dog in a harness and on-lead in case it has to be pulled aboard.

In the event of a drowning, the scent of the underwater victim will rise to the surface and drift along with the current. In a water search, the dog team must start downstream from the victim's point of entry and work upstream so that the scent is coming towards them. When working a dog from a boat, the handler must watch for the dog to stop alerting or to lose interest in the water. If this happens, turn the boat around and wait for the dog's first alert; this will indicate the point where the scent begins and that the body is in that area. Since underwater scent will drift out and away from the body, the search should be done in a circular pattern, starting from where the dog alerts and moving out to the sides and downstream. Depending on the water's current and conditions, the body is usually found within fifty feet of the alert.

CHAPTER SEVEN

Criminal Work

CRIME SCENES AND CRIMINAL SEARCHES

A ny search can lead to a crime scene. The mission may begin as a search for a lost or missing person and lead to the recovery of a murder victim or to evidence or result in the pursuit of a suspect.

There are dog handlers that specialize in criminal searches and crime scene work because it takes very specific knowledge and advanced skills to successfully work criminal trails, crime scenes and the pursuit of suspects.

CRIME SCENE EQUIPMENT

In a known criminal incident, the risk of personal injury increases dramatically; to reduce personal risk, handlers are advised to carry special equipment. A harness and lead of sub-dued color (black or gray) reduce visibility. The handler should wear appropriate clothing, particularly dark colors for night work. A flashlight with an amber or red night-vision lens to maintain night visibility and to minimize the beam works best. Work the dog on a shorter lead (four to six feet) and in a criminal pursuit when there is evidence that the suspect is in the area, use a traffic lead, two to four feet long, to keep the dog close to you.

Consider purchasing and wearing a ballistic vest. Ballistic vests, or body armor, are not bulletproof; resistant yes, but bullet*proof*, no. However, the vest is designed to absorb the impact of the shell and prevent the bullet from penetrating the vest. Such vests are rated by the manufacturer according to their ability to prevent penetration. Some vests are designed to protect the wearer against knives and other sharp instruments while others are designed to resist different kinds of bullets at varying distances. The ballistic vests on the market today are durable, lightweight and worth the money if the handler is seriously interested in criminal work.

CHECKING IN

Dog handlers must have a detailed understanding of crime scenes and the handling of evidence before responding to any type of search. Crime scenes must be carefully protected and volunteers must be careful not to touch or disturb anything at a crime scene. Just as handlers are frustrated when the scent article is contaminated, law enforcement agencies also become frustrated with the improper handling of evidence during a criminal case.

When the team arrives at the crime scene, the dog should be left in the vehicle until time to work. The handler will meet with the officer in charge and find out what needs to be done.

Law enforcement agencies' needs will vary, but most likely they will require that the dog team determine the trail of the suspect. The dog may find the trail to and from the crime scene and once the trail is found, the team may pursue the suspect. Teams can also be used to locate evidence or to find the entrance or exit point in a crime scene. The dog may be able to determine the movement of the suspect through the crime scene or possibly link the suspect to the scene or to evidence found. The dog may also be required to identify the suspect in a "line-up" situation.

When you arrive at the scene, meet directly with the officer-in-charge. Find out the type of incident and what the agency wants from the dog team. Find out if the suspect is armed with a weapon and if so, what kind. If there is a description of the suspect, write it down. Some handlers request that an armed officer be assigned to stay with them on the trail.

If possible, you will need to obtain and package the scent article that you will be using. Find out what articles are available, and choose one that has the least likelihood of contamination. Bloody clothing does not make a good scent article; the smell of blood will alter or overpower the original scent. Choose a scent article wisely.

If you must enter the crime scene itself to get a scent article, it is crucial that you enter and exit as quickly as possible. Avoid disrupting evidence and watch where you place your feet. Many crime scenes have been ruined by careless officers and workers who inadvertently wandered through blood stains, moved valuable evidence, snuffed out cigarettes or knocked things over.

Bring a scent article collection kit with you including some kind of collection tool as part of your gear. Don't assume that tools and a container will be available at a crime scene. Tell the officer-in-charge what item you want to use. Don't touch the article until it has been photographed or logged. Package the item, and leave the scene. Once you have the article from the crime scene, you are responsible for it. You may have to sign for it to maintain the chain of evidence.

Any officer that works with you must be instructed in what you expect him or her to do. Most officers will have very little, if any, experience in working with a Bloodhound but most are more than willing to comply with a handler's requests. Educating departments ahead of time pays off on searches. A written outline of instructions helps to minimize the delay.

If the agency requests that you pursue a suspect it is crucial that you have an officer work with you. It is the officer's job, not yours, to make the arrest if you find the suspect. Officers who work with you on the trail should be instructed to remain behind or beside you at all times to avoid distracting the dog or contaminating the trail. If the trail leads to a building or structure, stop and have the officer search the structure first. If the suspect is not located by the officer, proceed into the building with the dog. Work slowly and cautiously! Suspects may be hiding in areas that were already checked and cleared by an officer or other searcher!

The officer working with you should use a flashlight only when absolutely necessary since a flashlight will illuminate you while you work. If you must use a light, wear a headlamp or carry a flashlight with a subdued beam to reduce the risk of becoming a moving target.

Digger and I once worked a case in which a two-and-one-half-year-old girl had been kidnapped from her front yard. Troy, one of the deputies on the scene, was familiar with how search dogs worked and volunteered to stay with us as we worked through a small neighborhood. When Digger indicated great interest in a culvert Troy immediately walked into a nearby garage to get a rake. Despite other officers telling him that they had searched the culvert Troy honored Digger's nose and looked again. Troy raked the culvert where Digger was indicating and revealed the child's clothing right where the other officers claimed to have searched.

A criminal trail is an excellent place to carry a pocket-sized tape recorder to record notes and information as you are working. Get a voice-activated recorder; start recording the moment you give the starting command. Update the recorder every time you change direction, stop, recover evidence or find the suspect. Indicate street names, business names, vehicle descriptions or structure descriptions you pass as you work. If you successfully trail to a suspect, be sure to note the time, date and location. When it comes time to write your report, it will be much easier to reconstruct the scene if you have a tape recording of the activities of the search.

Crime scenes often include pools of blood, deceased persons and weapons. Keep the dog out of the crime scene itself, if possible. Start the dog at the edge of the crime scene and work away from it to prevent any accidental destruction or contamination. If a piece of evidence is needed for a scent article, be sure to sign for and control the item throughout the search. You are responsible for maintaining the chain of evidence.

In many criminal cases, the media will be anxious for a story but avoid them until you have clearance from the investigating officer. Most agencies require that all media releases be cleared. It is vital that only specific information be released to the media as the wrong information may cost a conviction.

Media personnel may try to follow you while you are working but request that the agency you are working for keep the media away. Media lights and commotion may contaminate the trail or distract the dog. Don't give anyone other than the investigating agency your address and phone number. You do not want this information reflected in the media so that the suspect has access to it.

Once an arrest has been made, the prosecutor or district attorney determines whether or not there is probable cause for charges to be brought against the suspect. If you contribute to evidence in the case, you will, in most cases, be contacted by the prosecutor. In many cases, you will also be contacted by the defense attorney. Get clearance before you release copies of your report or comment on the search to anyone other than the investigating agency or the prosecutor. Defense attorneys will contact dog handlers in an attempt to find a hole in the case but refer all calls to the agency investigating or prosecuting the case.

The court will require a detailed report of your trail starting with the call-out. Your report must accurately describe the scent article, how you obtained it, and how it was packaged. You will need to include where the trail started, how you started the dog, the direction of travel, and any stops, barriers or obstacles you encountered. Indicate how the dog alerted and what he found at the end of the trail. Describe specific details of the trail as well as the distance covered and starting, finish and actual time on the trail.

In any report, it is to your advantage to be detailed. If the case does not go to trial for months or even years, it will be easier and more reliable to have a detailed report to refer to during testimony. One of the biggest pitfalls for a dog handler is leaving out details which accurately describe the activities of the dog.

THE THEORY OF THE DOMINANT HAND

A carefully planned bank robbery is interrupted when a quick-thinking teller trips the alarm. Sirens in the distance cause the robbers to panic and they grab the bag of money and run out a rear door. Panic forces them to exit into an alley. The "get-away car" is parked in a side lot. Both robbers run out the back door, pause briefly and then turn right, going around the building and into the parking lot. Both robbers are right-handed.

Imagine taking a walk in an unfamiliar place and up ahead the road forks. If the roads appear similar, left-handed people will choose the left fork, right-handed people will choose the right fork. Walking through a field and turning around to go back, left-handed people will circle to their left, right-handed people will circle to their right. Plan? Coincidence? Unconscious decision?

There has been much discussion about the "theory of the dominant hand." While it is not strictly a scientific process that defines this behavior, it would *appear* that a person will follow the direction of their dominant hand whenever possible when making turns or changing direction. Mission reports dealing with lost persons, fugitives, mentally ill, despondent and suicidal people, as well as people who are frightened, being chased, and who react purely on the spot all seem to agree that it is an unconscious choice.

A person fleeing from a scene will follow their dominant hand when changing direction and making turns as long as they can. If the right-handed person is, by circumstance, forced to turn left, they will do so, uncomfortably, only until they can again make a right turn. At a "T" intersection a panicked suspect will generally turn right and follow his dominant hand.

It is interesting to consider the theory of the dominant hand as you approach crime scene work. Obviously, if the theory is predominantly true, it makes chasing suspects somewhat easier in that if we can determine their hand dominance we may be able to determine their direction of travel and, in effect, plot their path. However, this theory relates primarily to unconscious choices and some suspects will carefully figure out their escape plans and follow them meticulously. Escape plans themselves may subscribe to this theory as well, although not as neatly as the unconscious choices made in a panic.

I remember one case in which the suspect was scared away from the crime scene by gunfire and ran through the brush to the edge of a river, turned right and ran down the river bank, under a bridge and then along a fence. At an opening in the fence the suspect turned right, ran across a street and through a small orchard to a second fence. He went through the second fence to a road and turned right, running to the intersection where he was apprehended. His turns were all to the right despite the fact that a left turn was available in each situation. The suspect was right-handed.

This theory is also helpful in dealing with "regular" lost and missing persons in that a lost person will tend to follow the direction of their dominant hand in attempting to work through their confusion. If the person comes to a fork in the trail, chances are that they will follow their dominant hand, especially at night and in wooded terrain where visibility is limited.

In lost person cases the victim is interviewed as soon after the event as possible. Case after case reveals that the lost person started out with a plan but something happened to change it, demanding that the lost person improvise. Once the person senses that the original plan has been altered, they begin to employ instinct; this is what leads to the dominant hand theory.

As you put together your mission report form add a blank for hand dominance and ask the mission coordinator or the family if the person is right- or left-handed. In crime scene work, ask if a weapon was used and if so, in what hand was the weapon held? Which way did the person turn when they left the building or room? Remember that this theory applies to situations where choice is made *unconsciously*.

Recently a cowboy herding cattle to some corrals went missing. He had last been seen headed for some corrals to the north. The rider had been missing about nine hours when the call was made for help. At first light the search was mustered and as searchers were arriving we began to plot the area to be searched. The terrain was canyons, ridges and drainages. To the north and west were timbered hills with steep drainages; to the south the hills led to a highway several miles away. To the east the drainages gave way to a gentle slope down to the Columbia River.

The missing person was an experienced rider who was dressed poorly for the forty-degree–Fahrenheit overnight temperatures and he carried no food. He did not appear to have any medical problems. As I was listening to plans being made to search for this rider I asked which hand was dominant. The other search coordinator stopped and looked at me and said,

Working uphill along the road.
PHOTO BY KAY SCHMITT

"What difference does that make—he isn't writing his way out of this!" and the coordinator continued to plan his search to the north and south. The rider was right-handed. I explained the theory quickly, and begrudgingly the hasty team was sent to the east, which was to the right. The rider was located quickly *to the east* headed for the Columbia River. He had made a right turn and, according to the rider, *followed his gut feeling* and rode east. Coincidence? Human nature.

Obviously this theory can help determine the areas to be searched and in what direction the search should concentrate or expand. As you plot the search area keep in mind the dominant hand theory in dealing with turns and roads and changes in direction. Remember that the most critical crime scene clues are the ones that you can't see, can't photograph and can't put in an evidence bag!

YOGI

PHOTO BY KENT AND DONNA DANNEN

Jefferson County, Colorado sheriff's deputy Al Nelson obtained his first Bloodhound, Frontier Amelia Jo (Amy), when she was only eight months old. After she received the best schooling he could get for her, she followed Al into law enforcement. According to an article in the *Denver Post*[1] following her death in February 1995, Amy "found missing children, located drowning victims for grieving relatives and followed the scents of criminals near and far" as well as providing everyday companionship and "entertaining children when Al spoke at schools."

Amy helped solve a dozen murders and contributed to numerous crime investigations, and even appeared on *Unsolved Mysteries*, but she never received the publicity that Yogi, the Bloodhound that tracked the body of Alie Berrelez, received. Amazingly, at least to the public, Yogi followed Berrelez' scent along city streets, busy Interstate 70, and finally into a mountain canyon. Yogi obtained national recognition and has since been requested to work on many highly publicized crime cases. However, the *Denver Post* quoted Al Nelson as asserting that "it was Amy who taught Yogi everything he knows."

Interestingly, on the search pictured here in Rocky Mountain National Park, Yogi started toward the trail to Cub Lake during a search for a teenage suicide victim. He then veered and followed the trail out of the park, going back to where the teenager had come from. Later, relatives determined that the teenager was probably headed for Cub Lake. They asked a friend with a trained Australian Shepherd to search that trail. The Aussie located the body in less than an hour. Sometimes human reasoning and canine ability must work hand in hand.

[1]"Cop Bids Farewell to Little-known Law Enforcement Legend." K. Simpson, *Denver Post*, Feb. 16, 1995.

SECURING THE SCENE

Scent is the most overlooked and underestimated piece of evidence available in every case, criminal or rescue. Why? Because it is invisible. As a general rule, police training does not address scent as evidence. Responding officers often have no idea that they are walking over and contaminating the best piece of evidence they have for establishing a suspect's presence.

It is important that police officers and search and rescue coordinators be familiar with how to secure a scene before the dog team's arrival. Knowing how and what to preserve will increase the chances for success. Without proper training and detailed instructions, the crime scene or scent articles will be hopelessly contaminated, thereby lessening or eliminating the usefulness of the dog.

It is the handler's responsibility to teach the agencies the proper methods of finding, collecting and packaging a scent article. You will need to stress that a good article has not been handled, processed for fingerprints or exposed to carbon monoxide fumes. Make sure that the equipment necessary for collecting a scent article is available to the officer in the field and give them a graphic demonstration of how this will benefit them as well.

The first step in training law enforcement personnel is to explain how scent leaves the body and where it goes. Explain how scent constantly drifts from the body with the skin cells carried on the air current. The scent attaches to the ground, vegetation, or surrounding area and the speed and direction of the air movement will determine how far the scent will drift.

Air temperature and precipitation as well as ground conditions will further affect the scent. A very hot day with no air movement will evaporate scent much more quickly than a moderately breezy day. Similarly, moist ground will hold scent better than desert sand.

When there is a strong wind, the dog may trail parallel to where the person actually walked because the air movement wafted the scent to one side of the trail. It is not known how long scent will actually be present in a specific location, but exposure to heat, wind and ground conditions will all affect how concentrated the scent will remain.

SCENT ARTICLE INFORMATION

General information about scent articles must be conveyed. Information such as the laundering of an article of clothing or an article being handled by anyone other than the dog handler is important to obtain, since the effectiveness of the article is thereby limited. Improperly collected articles, improperly packaged articles and improperly transported articles complicate the issue.

The best scent articles are items of clothing that have been close to the skin. A shirt, pants, hat, pillowcase or bottom fitted sheet from the subject's bed make excellent scent articles. Other items that have been successfully used as scent articles include sleeping bags, car seats, steering wheels, coffee cups, purses and wallets, shoes, and suitcases.

Crime scenes have more obscure scent articles. Depending on whether they have been contaminated or not, window ledges, weapons, the victim's clothing, door jambs, door handles, and footprints are usable scent articles. If the handler is not able to choose and collect the article, the officer should choose the articles for the handler based on specific training and instructions. It is best and easier for the officer to allow the handler to choose the article, but it may not always be possible. Once the article has been chosen, determine whether or not the article has been contaminated. If the article has been handled by more than one person or by persons who are no longer at the scene, processed for evidence, or laundered, the article is not usable. If the article is heavily contaminated, it becomes a last-chance article.

Keep everyone away from the article you have chosen. Avoid leaning over the article during selection and collection. Remember that your scent is drifting from your body to the scent article. If you are collecting a scent article outside or in any place with air movement of any significance, remember to stay downwind of the article until it is safely and securely packaged. Once you have the article, you must have a means to collect it. A coat hanger (extended), wooden spoon, tire iron, stick or tool will work well for picking it up. A clean, inverted, non-deodorized trash bag will work for collecting the item.

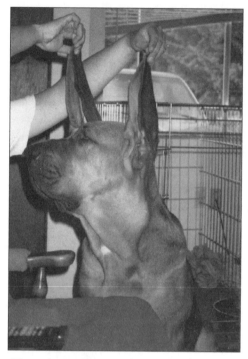

Those long ears cup the scent as the dog works. PHOTO BY JAN TWEEDIE

If anyone handled the article prior to packaging, that person must be present when the dog is started. The dog must eliminate the person from the scent article. The dog will check the person out and move on. If the dog does not move on, it may be necessary to find another scent article. This happens only when the scent article has been contaminated to the point of saturation with the other person's scent.

I remember one case where we were given a child's teddy bear, nicely collected and packaged in a plastic bag. When Digger was scented, he went over to the mother and sat down. In questioning the mother, she told us that she had washed the bear and had been holding it for the past 18 hours while her child was missing. The bear was saturated with the mother's scent, not the child's.

Describe the preferred methods of scent article collection and if the officer collects the scent article, he or she should turn the scent article over to the handler as soon as possible. If there is a chance that the article was contaminated, the officer should tell the handler right away. Several miles of trails have been wasted when it was discovered that the scent article had been contaminated and the team was following the trail of the wrong person.

EDUCATE

It is not only police officers that should be trained. Anyone who will be used in a search situation where a dog team will be utilized needs to be trained. This includes nursing home personnel, mental hospital personnel, and other search and rescue people. Nursing homes will often call when patients or residents wander away from the care facility. It is common for hospital staff to pick up and move residents' personal effects, so educate staff members ahead of time about scent articles and contamination.

One rainy night Digger trailed more than fifty blocks in search of an Alzheimer's patient who was finally located, deceased, less than a block away from the home. Why did Digger cover all that ground? The scent article had been contaminated when a member of the nursing home staff had changed the patient's bed. Digger was trailing the staff person who had changed the patient's bed an hour before our arrival and had gone home along the route that Digger trailed!

The first person on the scene should check the point of entry or departure for footprints. Footprints can often be successfully used as scent articles if they haven't been contaminated. Once this has been determined, the dog team must be called before the technicians process the crime scene. The police officer should secure the scene and stand away from the scent article until the team arrives.

In some cases there will be a vehicle pursuit ending with the suspect fleeing on foot. The officer should close the vehicle without tampering with or contaminating the inside compartment, and call for the dog team to gather scent from the inside of the car.

HANDLING EVIDENCE

Evidence is any item that will help to show who committed the crime or how the crime was done. Evidence includes weapons, body fluids, fingerprints and footprints. Dirt, scuff marks, tool marks and fibers from clothing or carpet are valuable evidence. Human hair, carpet fibers and body fluids can be chemically checked or scientifically examined to find out who or where they came from. Evidence can take a variety of forms. It can be as obvious as blood stains or as obscure as the scent of the fleeing suspect. Essential to any investigation are the prompt discovery and control of any item of value as evidence.

Specific information is written down when evidence is found. The name of the person who found the evidence, the exact place it was found, the time and date found and a description of the item are written in the officer's notes. The information attached to the item of evidence starts the chain of evidence. A chain of evidence is a written record. The record lists the name of every person that handled the evidence. The record also has all of the dates and the signatures of officers that handled or processed the evidence.

When the item is picked up and removed from the location it was found, the officer must log the time it was collected. The item is then secured in a bag or enclosure. This is to prevent decay and to make sure the item remains in the condition in which it was recovered. Many law enforcement agencies have officers that specialize in the collection and processing of evidence at crime scenes. The State of Washington has several laboratories staffed with highly trained technicians to assist in crime scene processing and evidence collection.

An identification tag is attached to the evidence. The evidence tag will have the case number, the officer's name who located or collected the evidence and the time and date when the evidence was collected written on it. Defense attorneys can get criminal charges dismissed, cases appealed and convictions overturned when the court finds out that crucial evidence was improperly gathered or mishandled between the crime scene and the courtroom.

When a dog team locates an item of evidence, the handler must tell the investigating agency immediately. Have the officer handle the item. Sometimes a dog handler will pick the item up, move it, inspect it or allow the dog to damage it before it can be logged in as evidence. If an item that might be evidence is found, the dog handler must tell the investigator.

Handlers should carry grid tape or surveyor's ribbon to mark the location of the item if found outside. Tie a length of ribbon to a nearby branch or brush. Do not touch the item. Leave the item exactly the way you found it. Have the investigating agency check the item. The officer will determine the item's value as evidence.

There will be evidence at every crime scene. At death scenes evidence recovery is crucial. There is evidence surrounding a body that should not be touched. A decomposed or decomposing cadaver scene has special evidence. The ground the body lies on becomes evidence in determining the length of time that the deceased person has been there. Footprints, animal paths, clothing and the soil in the area of the body are searched for their value as evidence.

Handlers should keep the dog out of the way of the scene once evidence is found. Officers will check for evidence in the area. Weapons and other large pieces of evidence which could be important to the case may be found away from the crime scene. Report your find, and move away from the area when an investigating officer arrives.

The chain of evidence continues every time the item is handled or moved. If the department wants the item dated or processed for fingerprints or chemicals, be sure there will be no chance that your fingerprints are all over the item. If you touch the item you will be fingerprinted to eliminate your prints. Handling evidence or destroying evidence in a criminal case is a crime. Be careful not to step on evidence. Stay out of the crime scene when possible.

If your team discovers evidence, you can expect to be called to testify. You will be asked how you found the item and what you did once you located it. Crime labs can run many different tests on evidence to determine the presence of fingerprints, chemicals, fibers, or blood stains. Any of this evidence can be crucial in gaining a conviction. If the item of evidence is sent to the crime lab for processing, the evidence tag is marked with the name of the officer sending the item, date sent and address and name of the lab that will be processing it. When the item is returned to the department the crime lab includes further information for the chain of evidence. The crime lab documents the name of the technician that processed the item, what was done to it, the type of evidence analyzed and the date it was returned. The evidence is placed in secure storage, or an evidence room, once it has been returned.

Evidence laws vary from state to state and handlers must

know the laws in his or her state. Known or possible evidence should be handled with care.

Some agencies will require the handler to keep the scent article between the time the trail was worked and the time the case goes to court. Other agencies will have the handler return the evidence to the agency to hold until the trial. If the handler is to maintain control of the item, it is crucial that the item is packaged properly and stored securely. Many handlers find that they are unable to secure the item in the manner in which evidence law requires and will request that the investigating agency preserve the scent article.

A scent article that is also an item of evidence must be stored in an airtight container to avoid the continued decomposition of the scent. It should be placed in a sealed container and labeled, then placed in a larger container, sealed and labeled as well. The label should list the crime, suspect, date found or used and the handler's signature.

Careful instructions must be given to the agency before the item is released if the agency wants it to be used again as a scent article. The handler should be the only person to handle the item because there can be years between the crime and the time the case goes to court. If there is a turnover of officers involved in the original crime scene and evidence collection period then this will ensure that the handler's scent is the only foreign scent on the item.

If the agency is planning to use the item as a scent article for a line-up or criminal identification, it is essential that the handler control the scent article. In these cases, keep the scent article frozen until it is used again.

If the handler maintains control of the evidence then the handler assumes liability for the item, including the article's preservation and safe delivery to the court. A handler that loses or destroys evidence may be destroying a vital part of the case. Some handlers will even use a locked freezer to store evidence.

The court will decide what happens to the evidence after the case is over and it may order that the item be returned to the original owner or to the agency investigating the case. In either case, handlers should not assume the responsibility for return of any item of evidence.

COURTROOM TESTIMONY

Every handler must prepare to testify in court if a search suddenly turns into a criminal case. Testimony requires that handlers keep accurate records; a handler that fails to do this can be easily discredited, and more than likely, embarrassed on the witness stand.

A dog handler should prepare well in advance of any possible testimony. From the first day the handler works the dog, records of training trails, demonstrations, missions and attendance at training should be kept. The goal is to present a comprehensive account of all the work that the team has done up to the point that the team was called to testify.

Bloodhound evidence is not universally accepted in courtrooms across the United States. Some states will readily accept it while others expressly forbid the use of Bloodhound evidence in any form. Other states will consider Bloodhound evidence on a case-by-case basis but will not convict a person of a crime based solely on Bloodhound evidence.

The court will ask how the dog was trained for trailing a person, who trained the dog and proof of training. Your written training records may be required by the court. Arrange with the court to allow you to provide copies of the records, certified, if they desire. The court will also need copies of your actual mission reports. Again, do not give them the original reports. These records are the foundation for establishing your credibility.

Many courts are unfamiliar with questions to ask a Bloodhound handler. Since training varies greatly between the German Shepherd and the Bloodhound, questions written for the examination of a German Shepherd handler will not be suitable for a Bloodhound handler. I have included a list of specific questions in this chapter that may be asked during a trial. Be prepared to answer a lot of questions. Courts allow dog handlers to bring a copy of their reports to remind them of specific details of the case but it is a good idea to rehearse the questions and the answers prior to appearing in court.

If you are subpoenaed to testify in court, ask to meet with the prosecutor to prepare your testimony. This will allow you to find out what will be asked by the attorney and assists the prosecutor in developing the case.

When called to the witness stand, answer all questions truthfully and briefly. Pause briefly before answering to give you time to calm down and think through the question. If you didn't understand the question, ask that it be repeated or rephrased. Don't give details that the question does not address. Most answers should be yes or no except for those questions that deal with how the dog trained and how the hound responded to the trail in the case. Be specific in these answers; generalizing leaves room for the opposing attorney to try to create doubt or turn the truth around.

When you testify in court, it is important to use terminology that is clear and nontechnical. Technical language may confuse the jurors or the judge so use familiar terms such as "trailing" in place of "pursuing," "following the trail" instead of a "scent path," and "find" instead of "locating the suspect."

Never make guarantees or false claims. Don't use the words "never" and "always" because they are too easily disproved. If you are caught lying or falsifying information you can be charged with perjury. In several states perjury carries a jail term or a substantial fine and it damages the credibility of everyone in the field.

Dress appropriately for the courtroom. A dog handler that testifies in court wearing blue jeans, coveralls, or unkempt clothing will lose credibility. Remember that you are testifying as an expert, so dress like one. A jury will be paying close attention to what you wear.

On rare occasions your dog may be subpoenaed to court with you. In the unlikely event that it is, make sure that the dog is bathed and well groomed. Carry a towel for wiping the dog's mouth and bring your working gear with you. Make sure that it is clean and presentable as it may be handled by the attorneys as well as the jury and the court. Leave the courtroom with the impression of professionalism.

Make sure that your report does not conflict with the police report by providing the investigating agency with a copy of your written report before court. Many law enforcement officers are unfamiliar with the working Bloodhound and they may misinterpret evidence found, the trail, or the reaction of the dog. By providing a written report, you are setting the record straight before you or members of the law enforcement agency testify.

If you retained the scent article used in the case, find out if it will be needed in the courtroom. You must be able to prove that the article has not been tampered with or altered in any manner. If the agency retained custody of the scent article as evidence, the agency must produce a completed chain of evidence and proper storage procedures. If you gave the agency instructions on proper storage for the article, provide these instructions in writing to the court.

Before testifying in court, tell the prosecutor or the attorney that called you if you have evidence. Be prepared to answer the questions asked of you by both sides. If you are planning to present a scent article as evidence or use it as part of your testimony, you will have to explain how the article was selected, obtained and handled to the judge and jury.

To assist handlers in preparing for courtroom testimony, teams should practice giving information in a courtroom setting. Normally the questions for handlers are given to the attorney who calls you to testify and the questions are designed to help establish your credibility as an expert witness.

There are court cases on record that establish the credibility of the Bloodhound and other tracking dogs. A handler that plans to work criminal cases should be familiar with them so check out your local law library or other handlers who may have compiled this specific information as well.

DEMONSTRATION TRAILS

Some dog handlers volunteer to run a trail for the jury, to demonstrate the dog's ability. This is a dangerous proposition. Regardless of the dog's ability, running a demonstration trail for a group of people who know nothing about the abilities of the Bloodhound can easily backfire. The pressure to succeed is immense and your credibility will ride on your success. I once watched a handler successfully testify in court who also volunteered to run a demonstration trail. The dog was distracted by the people following them and refused to work. The handler was discredited and the dog's evidence was dismissed.

COURTROOM QUESTIONS

1. Your name.
2. Where do you live? Your address. (I always give my work address. I do *not* want some convict to get my home address. Sometimes the city and state will suffice but ask the prosecutor *before* you testify).
3. Occupation. Be general.
4. When did you begin training Bloodhounds?
5. What breeds have you trained?
6. What kind of training do you do to learn to train dogs?
7. Do you hold any type of license for training dogs? Certificates? Proficiency rating?
8. Is a license required for training dogs?
9. What breed of dog was used in this case?
10. Is the dog purebred?
11. Is the dog registered with the American Kennel Club? (AKC registration papers *(a copy only)* should be submitted with your case file.)
12. Where is this dog registered?
13. How old is it?
14. What is its name?
15. How and where did you get the dog?
16. Who is the legal and registered owner of the dog?
17. How long have you had the dog?
18. Who is the dog's handler? Are there other people that handle the dog?
19. Of what clubs, groups, and professional associations are you a member?
20. How long have you been a member of each association?
21. Do any of the associations offer training?
22. How often are training sessions held?
23. How many training sessions have you attended?
24. What other types of training have you attended?
25. Where are the training sessions held?
26. What specific training sessions have you attended and what topics were covered? How are instructors credentialed?
27. How many times have you used this Bloodhound on criminal cases?
28. How many times have you used this Bloodhound for other kinds of cases?
29. On what other types of cases has this Bloodhound been used?
30. When an agency needs to contact you how do they call you out? What agencies have you assisted in the past year? Five years?
31. Are the dogs worked at any other time than on actual cases?
32. What records are maintained as to the working abilities of the dogs?
33. What form is used for your records?
34. What equipment is used in working a Bloodhound?
35. How do you start your Bloodhound on the trail of a person?

36. Have you trained this law enforcement agency regarding what to do when a Bloodhound has been called?
37. What will your Bloodhound do if he comes across a crowd of people in his trail?
38. Is your dog easily distracted by noises or traffic?
39. How does he react to gunfire?
40. Have you trained your dog to work in traffic, around moving vehicles? What does the dog do? Is he distracted?
41. How does he react to other animals?
42. Do you work this dog alone at all times? What does the dog do if there is more than one Bloodhound or working dog in the area? How does that affect his trail?
43. What was the date you were called out on this search?
44. How were you contacted?
45. Who called you?
46. Did you use your Bloodhound on this case? For what? Why was a Bloodhound used on this case?
47. What kind of case was this?
48. Where did you take the dog? Why there?
49. What was going on when you arrived?
50. When did you get there?
51. What kind of weather did you encounter at the start of the trail?
52. What was the approximate temperature?
53. What were the weather conditions the day before at the same location?
54. Where did you start the dog on the trail? Why there?
55. How did you start the dog? What did you use?
56. What is a scent article?
57. From where was the scent article obtained?
58. Who obtained the scent article?
59. How was it obtained?
60. How was it packaged? Is it possible that anyone else's scent could have been on the scent article when you started the dog? Were they present when the dog was started?
61. Was there anyone else near you and the dog when you started the dog on the trail?
62. Did you start the dog?
63. Where did the dog go? What kind of ground was it?
64. Where did the dog stop? What did the dog do?
65. Where the dog stopped trailing, who was identified? Why did the dog stop? Did the dog want to continue working?
66. What did you do with the scent article? Where is the scent article now? Has the scent article been handled since you used it?
67. Has this dog ever not found what he was looking for? Why? What have you done in training to work on those areas?
68. Have you received specific training in crime scenes or working dogs in a crime scene? Do you have certificates?

Sometimes the defense attorney will attempt to set up the trail to discredit the dog. If the defense or prosecution desires to watch the dog run a trail then be sure that *you* set up the demonstration. Use a runner that is reliable and familiar with the working Bloodhound. The trail should be short and to the point; adding obstacles only increases the chances of failure.

In some cases, the defense attorney may insist that the handler know nothing of the trail. While this is the correct assumption on actual missions, in practice the handler always knows something about the runner or the trail and you may need to remind them that a demonstration trail *is* a practice trail. If the defense attorney continues to insist then the handler should choose an experienced runner to lay the trail, limiting the distance to a quarter mile and making sure to select an uncontaminated scent article. Make sure they map the trail so that those following can see where the runner went and what path the dog is taking. Instruct the runner to make the trail basically straight and to avoid multiple obstacles. A demonstration trail has to be successful.

Limit the number of distractions by reducing the number of spectators. An alternative to the demonstration trail is to provide an original, unedited training video for the court.

When I am asked to run a demonstration trail I explain to the person requesting the trail that the dog has training records to show reliability; I would not expect him to prove his credibility any more than I would expect a doctor to prove himself before going into surgery. If the person wants more information about the working abilities of the Bloodhound I will happily furnish them with articles, books, and other related information.

CHAPTER EIGHT

Your Partner's Health

INJURIES AND ILLNESSES

Search dogs are exposed to a variety of hazards in the field and can be exposed to extreme elements for long periods of time. There are several medical books that will help you answer questions regarding the medical care of your dog. Some of the books I recommend are: *The Dog Owner's Guide to Home Veterinary Care, The Merck Veterinary Manual*, and *How to Have a Healthier Dog*. Your veterinarian may be able to suggest additional books for you.

WHAT IS NORMAL?

Many handlers are unsure what a dog's normal body temperature should be and few are aware of the correct range for heart rate and respiration. The chart on the next page indicates the normal values for a canine.

INFECTIOUS DISEASES

All search dogs must be routinely vaccinated to prevent general illnesses such as rabies, parvovirus, coronavirus, leptospirosis, canine infectious hepatitis, and distemper. In addition to these vaccinations, some veterinarians suggest that the dogs also receive a vaccination for bordetella. Vaccinating a search dog against Lyme disease is also to your advantage if you will be working in the wilderness. This is essential if you

---

NORMAL VALUES

BODY TEMPERATURE 102°F / 39°C

HEART RATE 100-130 beats per minute

RESPIRATIONS 22 per minute

---

live in the eastern United States or where there have been reported cases of Lyme disease. To make sure that your partner is protected, have the vaccination.

Annual vaccinations will prevent most diseases provided that the vaccinations are given on a regular basis. It is important that handlers keep excellent immunization records since proof of vaccination will be required before the dog is allowed on any commercial aircraft and may be a membership prerequisite in any search dog association.

Distemper: Distemper is a very contagious disease affecting both dogs and cats. The disease causes both physical and neurological problems in affected dogs and is caused by a virus which is passed through nasal and eye discharge. Symptoms include coughing or sneezing which transmit the virus into the air.

Parvovirus: Parvovirus primarily affects puppies and young dogs but an unvaccinated adult can easily become fatally infected. Parvo appears as a severe intestinal virus which is often mistaken for less severe illnesses in the first stages. The disease attacks either the heart (myocarditis) or the gastrointestinal tract (enteritis).

Coronavirus (Gastroenteritis): Similar to parvovirus, coronavirus is considered to be the less dangerous of the two. The disease is contagious and if left untreated, coronavirus can kill puppies and older dogs.

Leptospirosis: This is an infectious disease which is carried by rodents and spread through contact with infected urine, secretions or infected water.

Infectious Canine Hepatitis: This disease affects the liver and is highly contagious. There is a high fatality rate in puppies and young dogs and this is a difficult disease to treat.

External Parasites: Fleas cause a painful and unsightly rash and dermatitis and some dogs experience an allergic reaction.

There are numerous flea treatments on the market including collars, dips, bedding, shampoos, sprays, and powders. Pyrethrin-based products seem to be most effective against fleas. Use extreme care when applying any chemicals to your dog. Concentrated shampoos that are not properly diluted can poison the dog, so be sure to read the instructions on the label for proper use.

Chemical-based flea collars should not be used on scent hounds because the chemicals used to repel fleas can potentially interfere with a dog's scenting ability. There are herbal collars on the market that work well without affecting the nose.

Worms: Intestinal parasites, or worms, can be found in every dog. Dogs suffer their first infestation of worms shortly after birth and should be wormed at four weeks of age and then once every six months until they are a year old. Adult dogs should be routinely wormed once a year or more often if worms are detected in their stool.

To determine what type of worms are present, collect a portion of fresh stool and deliver it to your veterinarian for examination. The veterinarian will prescribe the correct worm medication based on the type of infestation.

Four basic types of intestinal worms affect dogs: roundworms, hookworms, whipworms and tapeworms. Heartworms are also prevalent in the southern United States and can now be found all across the nation. Search dogs that may travel into mosquito-infested areas should be placed on a monthly heartworm preventative under veterinarian supervision.

GENERAL MEDICAL PROBLEMS
OF THE BLOODHOUND

CONJUNCTIVITIS (Cherry Eye)
Runny eyes discharging a thick greenish or white mucus accompanied by red conjunctiva should be evaluated by your veterinarian. The eye may appear to have a protruding mass from the lower eyelid which is called the Harder's gland. With their loose eye skin, Bloodhounds in particular are prone to eye problems. Keep your hound's eyes clean and clear. I carry eyewash into the field, and during allergy and dry summer months, will frequently irrigate the eyes to keep them clear of dirt and dust. Many show handlers use a commercial eye drop that "takes the red out" but this only treats the symptom, not the problem.

Medicating the affected eye or eyes with an ophthalmic antibiotic is successful in some cases but treatment requires consistent application of the medication. Skipping medication may delay or prevent recovery without surgery. In those cases where antibiotic ointment is not successful it may become necessary to remove the Harder's gland. The surgery is relatively simple and requires a general anesthetic.

EAR INFECTIONS
Bloodhounds are prone to ear problems because the ear is so long and heavy that it traps moisture, preventing the ear from drying out. Prevent ear infections with regular ear cleaning and thorough drying.

SYMPTOMS: Rubbing the head along the ground, a strong odor from the affected ear, scratching at the ear, an internal ear color ranging from pink to bright red and/or a dark-colored discharge.

TREATMENT: Ear drops containing antibiotics and in some cases, oral antibiotics in conjunction with frequent cleaning while the infection is healing.

PREVENTION: Routine cleaning with a veterinary-approved ear wash. Consult with your veterinarian regarding the best cleaning solution and method. *Do not* stick ear swabs or place water in the ear for cleaning.

EAR HEMATOMAS

Puppies and adult dogs will occasionally experience a painful, blood-filled bruise on the ear. Long-eared dogs are frequent victims of this condition which is caused by a bite or blow to the ear. Puppies will often play "tag" by grabbing the long ear of another puppy in their teeth and dragging the puppy along. The hematoma will fill with blood and become a painful swelling.

TREATMENT: Releasing the pressure is the primary concern of the attending veterinarian and this is done either with a needle and syringe or through surgery, depending on the size of the hematoma. Antibiotics are often prescribed and an Elizabethan collar is useful to prevent the dog from scratching or irritating the injured ear.

CANINE HIP DYSPLASIA

Hip dysplasia is a debilitating hereditary problem affecting most large-breed dogs. It is a painful and progressive disease in which the head of the femur does not fit into the hip socket, or is not supported by the ligaments and slips out of joint. It is a painful and crippling disease that will cut short a working dog's career.

Reputable breeders have their hounds' hips X-rayed and evaluated by the Orthopedic Foundation for Animals (OFA) as well as subscribing to careful breeding programs. Select your breeder carefully when buying a puppy and have X-rays taken early. The OFA will only certify hips on dogs that are at least twenty-four months old.

SYMPTOMS: Difficulty in getting up; when the dog is running it appears to be hopping with both hind legs; pain in the joints; swaying; difficulty in climbing stairs; and lack of stability in the rear when pressure is applied. Diagnosis is made through X-rays.

TREATMENT: Pain medication, swimming, and restricted exercise. Some handlers recommend increased amounts of Vitamin C which may assist in strengthening the connective tissue and ligaments in young animals. Aspirin helps to manage the pain; however, aspirin can induce gastric distress and irritation. There is no cure for CHD and for most dogs the end result is euthanasia. Some handlers will invest in total hip replacements for the dog, but the cost is extremely high, the recovery period is long and slow, and there is no guarantee that the surgery will be successful.

PREVENTION: Careful breeding will limit the affected dogs; however, dogs with good hips can still produce dysplastic puppies. Some breeders start puppies on oral Vitamin C and keep the puppies on the vitamin throughout adulthood. A good diet that inhibits rapid growth combined with routine exercise such as swimming and walking will help build strong joints.

LYME DISEASE

Lyme disease is a real field hazard for both dog and handler and working in wilderness areas puts search dogs at high risk for this inflammatory disease. Lyme disease is primarily carried by the deer tick and it can easily be transmitted to the handler through a bite by the same tick.

SYMPTOMS: Stiffness in the joints, moderate swelling and arthritis-like symptoms. Pain is commonly experienced when the affected limb is handled, although examination by a veterinarian may not reveal any infection.

TREATMENT: Antibiotics may be beneficial. Pain medication and anti-inflammatory drugs are often given as well.

PREVENTION: Carefully examine your dog for ticks before, during, and after any time spent in the field. Use tick and flea repellants. Routine tick checks should be performed even at home. If a tick is located it should be carefully removed (including the head) and taken to the veterinarian to determine if the tick is the type responsible for the spread of Lyme disease. An annual two-shot-series vaccination is highly recommended for wilderness search dogs.

ARTHRITIS

Arthritis can occur in any dog, but search dogs and other working dogs are more likely to develop arthritis as a result of trauma, joint stress and accidents. Arthritis also develops in malformed joints and is present in most elderly dogs. It is a progressive and crippling disease and in most cases it is also very painful as the joint deteriorates.

SYMPTOMS: Pain upon rising or lying down, refusal to climb stairs or work in steep terrain, refusal to jump or work on obstacle training, and whimpers or cries of pain when the joint is manipulated. The dog may hold up the afflicted limb. Diagnosis is usually made with X-rays and through physical examination. Without clear X-rays it is nearly impossible to determine the extent of the disease.

TREATMENT: Pain medication, anti-inflammatory drugs, and hydrotherapy will occasionally benefit the animal. As the disease progresses the affected limb will become stiff and may become unusable.

TRAUMA AND SUDDEN ILLNESS

ACCIDENTS

Accidents usually result in puncture wounds, lacerations and fractures, burns, frostbite, electrical shocks, gunshot wounds, impaled objects and insect stings. Most accidents can be avoided with careful handling; however, there are those which are unavoidable. The key to a quick recovery is to minimize the risks and maximize the response to an injury once it has occurred.

FRACTURES

Fractures occur most commonly when a dog is hit by a car or sustains a fall. Caution must be used when handling *any* injured animal. Regardless of how much the dog loves you, pain means defensive behavior. Be mindful that the dog may strike out at you as you assess an injury. I carry a small roll of gauze in my pack to use as a muzzle if needed.

SYMPTOMS: Fractures may be obvious as when a bone protrudes through the skin or it may appear that part of a limb is out of alignment. Bone ends may be felt through the skin and the limb will be useless to the animal. A broken limb will move freely and appear distorted. Swelling around the fracture site will begin very quickly, the animal will be in obvious pain. If the break is an open fracture there may be bleeding at the wound site.

TREATMENT: The dog must be examined and treated by a veterinarian as quickly as possible. X-rays will reveal the seriousness of the fracture and will determine the route of care that will be most effective. Fractures can be set under a local or general anesthetic and placed in a cast. In more complex fractures the veterinarian may have to operate to place pins, plates or screws over the fracture site to make sure that the bone ends knit properly. Surgical repair necessitates a carefully supervised recovery period and a casted limb needs to stay clean and dry.

It is possible that a dog can return to the field following careful and complete treatment of a fracture. I know of a Bloodhound that broke her hind leg as a young dog but after careful treatment not only finished her show championship but also completed both an Instinct Certification Test and completed the Mantrailer level of the Trailing Trial Standard and she returned to the field as a working search dog.

DISLOCATIONS

A dislocated limb is excruciatingly painful and appears distorted and out of alignment with the dog's body. Hip joints are the most common site for dislocation and they will usually occur following a jump or fall.

SYMPTOMS: The dog may carry the affected limb which may appear shorter than the normal side.

TREATMENT: The limb can be returned to the socket fairly easily by a veterinarian. This should never be attempted by an untrained person since reducing (replacing) a dislocated limb requires that the dog be given a muscle relaxant or general anesthetic. If the dislocation occurs repeatedly or if the limb does not easily return to the socket, it may be necessary to pin the limb. I remember a search in which Kady and I were trailing a rape suspect down a steep embankment when I slipped and went tumbling down the hill with Kady rolling alongside me. At the bottom Kady stood up and cried out. Immediately her front leg was up and her foot was dangling.

A quick examination led me to believe that she had hurt her shoulder but that it wasn't broken. I cautiously moved it a little and heard a loud "CLICK!" Kady immediately quit crying and licked my face. Later, the vet X-rayed the shoulder and said she may have partially dislocated it in the tumble and when I manipulated the limb, it popped back. We were lucky. Rest and a little Butazolidin took care of the inflammation and Kady was back in the field in no time.

BURNS

Burns can occur quickly and can result in painful and untreatable conditions. Burns occur when the dog is scalded by a hot liquid or exposed to flames in a fire-rescue situation. Although dogs are naturally cautious of fire there have been numerous dogs injured by it.

SYMPTOMS: Obvious burns, soot, open wounds and pain. The handler usually witnesses the incident and can easily determine the wound site.

TREATMENT: Third-degree burns that expose underlying tissue and cover more than 25 percent of the body are almost always fatal and the dog should be euthanized to prevent suffering. Second-degree burns covering a small area of the body, or first-degree burns, can be treated with cool packs and antibiotics (infection is the major killer in burn victims). The hair should be shaved away from the burn and cool packs applied as soon as possible following the accident. The dog should be treated for shock and monitored to ensure plenty of fluid intake.

In serious burn cases it is necessary to place the dog on intravenous fluids and antibiotics. Special burn dressings can be applied and pain medication or topical anesthetic can be given to minimize the pain. Burns must be kept clean during the healing process.

ELECTRICAL SHOCKS AND INJURIES

Puppies are the primary victims of electrical accidents caused by playing with or chewing on electrical cords, so pay close attention to what a puppy chooses as a teething object. It is a good idea to tape electrical cords to a baseboard or up the wall out of reach of the puppy to prevent accidents.

SYMPTOMS: Burn or scorch marks, coma, and seizures. Wounds can be treated as a burn (see above) but should be evaluated by a veterinarian. Severe burns often result in coma, neurological damage and death.

TREATMENT: Wounds are treated by cleaning, debridement (clearing away burned and dead tissue) and in some cases pain medication. Restraining the dog to prevent chewing or biting the wound is essential.

FROSTBITE

Winter searches with exposure to harsh, frozen conditions can easily result in frostbite. Frostbite can become very serious and cause the loss of a limb if it is not recognized and treated immediately.

SYMPTOMS: The limb appears pale in the initial phases and when closely examined will reveal poor circulation; the limb will feel very cold to the touch and the dog will have no immediate capillary refill or pain reflex. In later stages the limb will be very painful and swell.

TREATMENT: Frostbite must be evaluated by a veterinarian. In the field, however, you can begin gentle re-warming efforts starting with tepid packs and gradually moving to warmer packs every ten to fifteen minutes until the limb circulation returns to normal. *Use caution:* As the limb re-warms there may be a great deal of pain involved and it may be necessary to muzzle the animal to prevent an instinctive reaction. Severe frostbite may necessitate amputating dead tissue.

HYPOTHERMIA

Hypothermia is the term given the decline in body temperature caused by exposure to frigid temperatures and wind chill factors coupled with cold temperatures or submersion in near-freezing water. Hypothermia can be fatal and many humans succumb to hypothermia every year.

For those searchers who respond in winter conditions hypothermia is a real concern. Every search dog team should include a designated person whose job on every winter mission is to assess hounds and handlers for this deadly affliction. Pay attention to those searchers around you and watch for signs and symptoms!

SYMPTOMS: Stumbling, staggering, confusion, slowed reactions and lagging behind are all symptoms of hypothermia. When the body begins to lose heat the blood flows to the body's core to keep the vital organs functioning. Limbs may become useless. Slight hypothermia is classed as a body temperature between 85-90°F, and serious hypothermia is declared when the body temperature drops to or below 60°F.

TREATMENT: The dog must be re-warmed. Using blankets, hot water bottles or a warm bath, slowly begin to re-warm the dog. As the body temperature climbs the dog will become more active but make sure that the dog stays warm. In severe hypothermia, warmed IV's are started or heated fluids are lavaged into the abdomen.

PREVENTION: Keep a critical eye on your working dog when working in extremely cold temperatures combined with wind, snow or cold water. Never put a wet dog into an open, moving vehicle; exposure to the cold and wind could result in hypothermia.

HYPERTHERMIA

Hyperthermia, the opposite of hypothermia, means that the body's core temperature has risen dangerously high. Hyperthermia is caused by prolonged exposure to high temperatures or direct sun.

SYMPTOMS: Lack of coordination, muscle weakness, tremors, increased heart rate and panting. The dog may stagger, vomit or have diarrhea and the mucous membranes in the mouth may become bright red. At 109°F the dog will begin to suffer neurological injury and can die.

TREATMENT: Rapid access to a veterinarian. In the meantime, the dog must be cooled. Use a hose, cold packs, or wet towels packed around the stomach and head, or immerse the dog's body in cool water. Continue the cooling process and seek veterinary care immediately, checking the temperature frequently.

PREVENTION: Frequent cooling rest breaks on searches in hot and dry areas. If there is a creek or water nearby, walk the dog into the water at least belly deep. If a hose or spray bottle is available, spray the dog down during each rest break. Avoid searching during the heat of the day if early mornings or evenings are an option. Keeping close watch over the dog's reactions and abilities will help you catch the first signs.

BLOAT

Bloat is the distention of the stomach due to excess gas. If the gas becomes trapped the stomach will distend and the dog will be in obvious distress. Torsion occurs when the stomach rotates under the pressure of the trapped gas and the end or ends of the stomach become pinched. Gangrene can set in and the dog can die quickly. Bloat is caused by many things but is most often attributed to overeating, consuming a great deal of water following a meal or exercise, heavy exercise following or just prior to eating, stress or trauma. Bloat can also be caused by ingesting rocks or similar objects.

I had just returned home from a search in Eastern Washington and all was well upon my return. I took a shower and when I stepped out not ten minutes later, Kady was standing in the bathroom in obvious distress. Her abdomen had ballooned to such an extent that I could barely get my arms around her. I called my vet and told him that I was on my way with a bloating Bloodhound.

The vet took one look at her and grabbed a stomach tube to try to relieve the growing pressure and to prevent Kady's death. The tube wouldn't go down into Kady's stomach, which meant that Kady was torsioning; Kady was dying.

The vet then took a large-bore needle and plunged it through Kady's side and into her abdomen. There was a rush of air as the pressure was released. We got an IV started in her leg as she went into shock. I stepped back while he took X-rays and went over her. It was a long thirty-minute wait.

The X-rays showed that Kady had a cardiac torsion. This meant that her stomach was twisted on the upper end, closest to her heart. Without surgery she would die. This local vet did not do this type of surgery and told me I had to get her to a specialist. I loaded a drugged but conscious Kady in my Blazer and drove thirty miles to a pet emergency clinic where there were vets who could do the surgery. By the time we got there Kady had bloated again and was very sick. The veterinarian performed the surgery and relieved the bloat and torsion. To prevent her from ever torsioning again he performed something called a gastropexy. A gastropexy requires that the surgeon take a flap of the stomach muscle and wrap it around one of the ribs, suturing it in place. With this surgery the dog can bloat again but the stomach is anchored and can not torsion again, which is the major killer.

Kady stayed in the emergency hospital for five days. I brought her home and spent another five days caring for her, and against all odds, she made it. It took two weeks to get her to eat, but soon she was back to her feisty self. Veterinary costs were more than $1,600 just for the emergency care and surgery and there was no guarantee that the dog would live. Bloodhounds are very prone to bloat and torsion.

SYMPTOMS: Panting, obvious distention of the belly, stomach pain, excessive slobbering, gagging, the inability to keep water down, increased heart rate, pale mouth membranes and shortness of breath. The stomach will have a hollow sound when tapped.

TREATMENT: Immediate veterinary care is mandatory. Reducing the pressure in the stomach is essential and requires emergency treatment. The dog must also be treated for shock.

Major surgery requires a quiet and closely supervised recovery period. Many dogs do well following bloat or torsion surgery provided that they are well cared for and that all medications are given as directed. A bland diet will be required for approximately one week following surgery if there are no complications.

PREVENTION: Do not exercise your dog within two hours of eating. Some handlers use acidophilus powder or yogurt to stimulate intestinal flora and decrease gas problems while other handlers feed dry food that contains no corn or ash products. Still others withhold water following a meal to prevent excess drinking. Do not feed the dog and leave it unattended but check on it frequently following feeding. Bloat caused by overeating tends to set in within three hours following the meal and often much faster.

Do not feed the dog immediately before or after working or transporting. Avoid feeding the dog during the hottest portion of the day; evening or early morning feeding is best. You can also soak the dog food for fifteen to twenty minutes before giving it to the dog to allow the dry food to absorb water and release the air before the dog swallows it. Another method is to feed the dog in an elevated dish to prevent swallowing air.

FOREIGN BODIES

Puppies and some adult dogs will pick up and swallow almost anything. One day Kady came up to me whining and pawing at my hands. She refused food and was restless. Her stomach was a little sore to the touch and she became more agitated over the next half hour. Emergency surgery revealed five rocks in her gut, one of which was the size of a large egg! The vet closed her up with 108 stitches and it took megadoses of antibiotics, sedatives, fluids and love to pull her through.

SYMPTOMS: Agitation, retching, vomiting, whining, pawing at the stomach.

TREATMENT: Immediate veterinary intervention. The objects will be seen on most X-rays. Surgery is usually required to remove the objects. Many dogs will continue to swallow rocks and other things which may result in multiple surgeries or death. Handlers have tried muzzling the dog whenever it is outside; careful observation, clearing all rocks and articles out of the dog area or placing the dog on a cement surface may help.

EMERGENCY CARE IN THE FIELD

The handler is often faced with providing minor first aid in the field. Injuries are usually limited to lacerations, abrasions, puncture wounds, and bruises. First aid should consist of cleaning, applying an antibiotic cream or ointment, bandaging and transporting to a veterinarian for care. In more serious injuries such as fractures, dislocations, severe lacerations, abrasions, bruises or contusions, hypothermia or hyperthermia, the handler should do only what is necessary to immobilize the animal and get the animal to a veterinarian for immediate care.

Handlers should remember that a dog can be treated with almost any human medication; on-site paramedics or other emergency medical personnel may be a resource for the proper supplies. Advanced medical support such IV fluids, setting or casting a fracture or similar serious medical considerations should be left to a veterinarian. Use your radio to contact help and have the mission coordinator arrange for a veterinarian to be contacted and ready for your arrival.

Snake and insect bites and stings pose another potentially serious field medical problem. These can be fatal to a dog that does not receive quick treatment so pay close attention to insect stings and bites and check the dog over for any signs of an allergic reaction.

Digger and I were on a search in the foothills of the Cascade Mountains when he stumbled upon a nest of bees on the trail. Both of us were stung several times and both of us required emergency medical treatment. I now carry a sting kit on every search.

Symptoms of an allergic reaction range

A picture of Bloodhound health.
PHOTO BY JAN TWEEDIE

from a rash or irritation at the site of the sting or bite to shortness of breath, hives (bumps), swelling of the site or swelling of the windpipe and difficulty breathing. Emergency care will be necessary.

Snakebites do not occur very often, although a great many searches take place in snake territory. More often the dog will trail over the snake and the handler will be the one who gets bitten. You should carry a commercial snake bite kit in your field pack and you should be very familiar with how to use it. Consult with your veterinarian to learn the proper emergency response. The human anti-venom can also be used on the canine searcher. It is very important for the veterinarian to know what kind of snake was involved, the time of the bite and your medical response to the bite in the field.

SHOCK

In any accident or injury, illness or trauma, the dog must be treated for shock. Shock can also be caused by a low level of electrolytes and fluids which occurs in hyperthermia. Shock can kill, so it is imperative that you know the signs and symptoms.

SYMPTOMS: Cold extremities, pale mucous membranes, confusion, staggering, lethargy, depression and fear.

TREATMENT: Fluids, steroids, pain medications, cortico-steroids, and maintenance of body temperature. The treatment for shock requires veterinary care.

FIELD FIRST AID KITS

A canine first aid kit is a must for every handler. Some of the items may require a veterinarian's prescription or assistance in obtaining them. Work with your veterinarian to stock your kit with medications and first aid equipment relevant to your dog, your training and experience and the areas in which you will be searching. A suggested canine first aid kit can be found in Chapter 3.

Moleskin can be used in the field to close cuts on pads, legs, and some major skin tears until the dog can be evaluated by a veterinarian. The main drawback to moleskin is that the wound can become infected and the moleskin may be difficult to remove without acetone. *Do not* use this method unless you have received guidance and training from your veterinarian.

CHAPTER NINE

The Working
Search Team

Most law enforcement agencies are vaguely familiar with
working dogs but they are usually only exposed to
aggression-trained, protection and building search dogs. Some
police dogs are used for tracking but only on a very limited
basis. Many police officers will not try to track a suspect if the
trail is more than two hours old.

This is where the trained search dog comes into the picture
and where training and practicing on old trails pays off. Any
handler who hopes to be called out on a mission must be prepared to demonstrate the abilities and capabilities of the team.
Handlers must assess whether they are ready to respond to a
call-out. Teams that are ready must be able to answer yes to
the following questions:

1. Am I in good physical condition?
2. Is my dog in good physical condition?
3. Can my dog make a find on a trail that is at least 24 hours
    old at least 85% of the time?
4. Can my dog find the subject on a trail less than 24 hours
    old at least 90% of the time?
5. Do I have detailed documentation of all of my training
    trails?
6. Do I have the minimum field equipment and clothing nec-
    essary to respond?

7. Can I read my dog and his or her actions and alerts clearly and without reservation?
8. Do I have the necessary dog equipment and transportation?
9. Do I trust my dog to follow a trail I cannot see in a situation that I cannot control?

DEMONSTRATIONS AND QUALIFYING CRITERIA

When setting up a demonstration trail, you want as many of the variables to be in your favor as possible. It is crucial that the demonstration trail be successful for the dog team, and an elaborate trail, a long trail or a very old trail has a tendency to backfire.

A typical demonstration trail is two hours old, and one-quarter to one-half mile long. A trail laid in the shape of the letter "j" or a question mark in open terrain or a lightly forested area is best. Avoid running a demonstration trail that is more than four hours old even though you may know that your dog can handle a twenty-four hour old trail easily. Don't practice in the same area before the trail to avoid confusing the dog or contaminating the area. Use a simple scent article, a T-shirt or similar clothing item, properly collected and packaged. This is not the time to demonstrate the sterile swab scent article.

The dog's trailing style should be explained to the observers before the trail is started. A short explanation of scent articles and how the dog is started is important. Instruct the observers to stay behind you and to be as quiet as possible to avoid distracting the dog.

I often use the head of the agency as the runner and carefully explain what we want him or her to do. It's very convincing to have a sheriff or police chief hiding from the dog and to have the dog find them, but make sure they know to stay put at the end of the trail.

Some search and rescue organizations require that the handler prove his or her abilities and may stage a qualification trail for the dog to work. Be sure that the testing group knows how your breed works before the trail is laid and make them aware of the limitations of the dog as well.

Some organizations establish criteria for dog and handler qualification. The team must meet the criteria before they are qualified to respond to an actual search and rescue call-out. The basic qualification criteria for any dog team should be the ability to work a twenty-four-hour-old trail that is at least one and one-half miles long. The trail should have one crossing runner (someone who crosses and contaminates the trail at one point), and the dog must identify the correct person at the end of the trail. The crossing runner must wait at the end of the trail close to the runner the dog is seeking. The trail must be completed within ninety minutes of the starting time. The dog that is unable to accomplish this usually requires additional training.

Some organizations may require the team to complete the trail in one hour. Natural obstacles such as roads, ravines and water crossings are built into these trails to simulate common search conditions. The runner's trail typically follows a natural wandering path with at least one change of direction, closely resembling the pattern of movement of a lost person.

Three tests or qualifying trails can be set up for proving reliability. The first level of testing should involve a trail that is one and one-half miles long through brushy terrain. The trail should be no less than four and no more than twelve hours old. The dog should be able to complete the trail in less than one hour but many dogs will be able to finish in less than thirty minutes.

The second level should be longer in distance through more dense terrain and should include water or some similar obstacle for the dog to cross or bypass. The trail should be at least twenty-four hours but no more than thirty hours old. This time frame allows the dog team to simulate a standard missing person case in which a team is called the day after a person's disappearance.

The third level of testing includes terrain changes, water, roadways, and dense ground cover. This trail should be at least one and one-half mile long but no more than three miles long. This simulates the toughest kinds of wilderness searching. The trail should be at least twenty-four but no more than thirty-six hours old. Wind and terrain conditions should be considered when evaluating the dog's performance.

If the primary response area is desert or extremely dry and dusty, the qualification trails should mirror these conditions. A dry area is more difficult to work because scent does not remain long in dry or dusty areas, so the age and length of the trail in these test situations should be shorter.

Training and testing scenarios should also include varying temperatures, varying scent articles, contamination of trails and scent articles and precipitation. Although rain or snow can't be simulated, training and testing in these conditions should be done whenever possible if they are elements that will be found on a search. If the team will be working on city searches, at least one of the trails should be worked where traffic, people, buildings and similar elements will be encountered.

Each of the test trails should be judged by two people who are proven handlers of the breed being tested. The judges should evaluate the team's ability to follow the trail and should provide written feedback following the conclusion of the trail. Feedback should include overall performance and a detailed map of the trail indicating the runner's trail overlaid by the dog's trail. The judges should also comment on the attitude and ability of both the dog and the handler. A judge is evaluating the team's capabilities, not the individual dog, the breed or the handler. Personal bias has no place in the field.

Equipment should be closely examined for field readiness during testing. The handler should wear field gear during all testing trails to get used to wearing it and working the dog at the same time.

To help determine when a team is ready for call-out or qualification, the handler must be able to answer "yes" to all of the following questions:

1. Am I physically ready to spend a night in the field?
2. Do I have the proper equipment for the field?
3. Did my dog make a positive find on at least three judged qualification trails that were at least twenty-four hours old and one and one-half miles long?
4. Was the terrain in the qualification trails varied and consistent with wilderness searching?

5. Did the dog clearly identify the runner at the end of the trail?
6. Do my training records show all successes and failures? Are the records ready for a judge's evaluation?

A team that is ready for call-out should be physically and mentally sound and they should have enough stamina to stay out in the field for long periods of time. A handler that is physically incapable of working less than four hours without a break or covering less than five miles is physically unfit for wilderness searching. Such a team may be able to work short distance searches, but it will depend on the team's training. The judges who qualify search dog teams must be willing to say, without hesitation, that the team is ready to respond when a life depends on it. If there is any doubt then the team is not qualified.

Agencies want a reliable resource to respond to their needs. Being reliable means you will respond when called and that you will follow through when you make a commitment. You may not be able to respond to every call; prior commitments in your life make this an unreasonable expectation. Some call-outs will be for a kind of case that you have chosen not to work or one in which you have no training, such as cadaver recovery or crime scenes. Make these choices before the call comes and let the dispatching agency know well in advance of any limitations that you may have.

The working team.
ILLUSTRATION BY CRYSTAL MELVIN.

I have talked with some agencies to find out why they refuse to call a search dog team. The most common response is that the dog team is just overlooked; too many things are happening at once. But I've also been told stories about handlers that claim wonderful abilities, but when put to the test, they can't deliver the goods. They may complain about contaminated scent articles or about poor weather and trailing conditions. Or it may take too long for the team to get to the site of the search or the handler comes ill equipped to work. These excuses will only frustrate agencies and other SAR teams.

Exposure will help make agencies aware of your team so contact schools in your area and offer to give talks or a demonstration for the students about search dogs. Scout groups and other public service groups make excellent audiences. Prepare a written resume for your search team and circulate it to the agencies in your area. Business cards can further reinforce your presence. Be patient. Getting in the door is half the battle!

TRAVELING WITH THE SAR DOG

CAR TRAVEL

During the course of a puppy's basic training, car travel is the first step in familiarizing the young search dog with moving vehicles. Start in the very beginning making traveling by car a regular event in the puppy's life. Practice rides make this training easier for the dog and acquaint the dog with the starts and stops of a car.

When transporting the dog for the first few times, make sure that the dog is confined in a crate or a box. Some dogs will panic when the car begins to move while others will become carsick and may vomit. Confining the dog in a crate in the car makes good sense. In car accidents a dog is more likely to suffer blunt trauma from being hurled into the driver, dashboard or sides of the vehicle if he is allowed to wander freely. Placing the dog in a sturdy carrier will prevent those kinds of injuries. An unrestrained dog may also escape from the vehicle if a door is left open and most will panic and run if there is a car accident.

Once you are confident traveling short distances, take the dog on longer adventures, stopping frequently (every two hours or so) to walk the dog and show him the new sights. Carry a non-spill water dish in the car along with a gallon of water from home to refresh the dog along the way. If the dog does get carsick, consult your veterinarian regarding appropriate anti-nausea medications. Beware of sedatives which will affect the dog's working ability. Most dogs get used to traveling by car after the first few trips, and the dog will soon link the car ride with working.

COMMERCIAL AIR TRAVEL

As the general public has become more aware of search dogs and the service they provide, a movement has started to formally recognize search dogs as "Public Service Dogs." This title would afford the certified search dog teams the same access and privileges given to seeing-eye dogs and support dogs, such as allowing search teams to fly on commercial aircraft with the dog flying in the passenger compartment instead of in the baggage section.

Preparing for flight.
PHOTO BY JAN TWEEDIE

Digger and I once responded to a search by commercial airline and when I made my reservation, I informed the ticket agent that I would be flying a Bloodhound and expressed my concerns for his well-being. When the agent learned that Digger was a search and rescue dog, the conversation changed from "He will be just fine in the baggage compartment," to "I will make sure you have a bulkhead seat so he can stretch out." This particular airline officially recognizes search dogs and allows the dog to fly with the handler in the passenger compartment.

There are those passengers that will object to a canine passenger; however, the airlines that do endorse search dogs will usually deal with the conflict quickly and efficiently. Once the passengers learn the reason why the dog is on the plane, comments, compliments and lots of questions usually follow. Be sure that dogs are clean and "presentable" to the eye and nose before flying them in the passenger cabin. The impression you leave must be a good one.

HELICOPTER SAFETY

SAR dog teams must remember that the helicopter pilot is the person in authority on the aircraft. It is the pilot that is responsible for the success or failure of the mission as well as the safety of the crew and passengers and so the directions of the pilot or crew must be strictly adhered to in order to ensure the safety of the teams.

Handlers should place the dog on a short traffic lead (eighteen inches long) and maintain tight control of the dog at all times. The teams must remain at least 100 feet away from the helicopter unless boarding or directed to approach the craft by the pilot or designated crew member.

Eye protection, goggles or a handkerchief, should be used to protect your eyes from flying dust, gravel or sand. If you do not have eye protection, move at least 150 feet from the landing zone and turn your torso away from the approaching craft, leaning over slightly to prevent injuries to your eyes. The dog's eyes should be protected as well by covering his eyes with your hands or a cloth. Some dogs will struggle if they cannot see what is making all the noise as the helicopter approaches so practice this technique during training to determine the most effective method.

Handlers should carry and wear protective headgear. Climbing helmets are perfect and should be put on and secured with the chin strap well before the helicopter arrives . Loose caps or clothing must be secured prior to the approach and landing of the chopper.

Approach the chopper only from the front to maintain visual contact with the pilot. When leaving the helicopter move along the side to the front or according to the directions of the briefing officer. *Never* approach the tail rotor of the craft.

Never approach or attempt to board the chopper without the knowledge and permission of the pilot! Packs, gear bags or other equipment should be secured on the ground with nothing sticking up in the air more than the height of the handler. Handlers should make sure that small items are securely held or fastened to packs before the craft arrives to prevent the rotor wash from picking the items up and causing damage or injury.

When walking towards (approaching) a helicopter you must incline your body forward (bend at the waist). When leaving a chopper maintain the same inclined position to prevent injury or accidents. Equipment loaded on the chopper must be secured. Crates should be tied down to the gear racks. The crew on the chopper will take care of this for you. If your dog is to be crated during the flight make sure that the crate is secured appropriately and the door is latched properly.

Everyone on the chopper must be familiar with the communications method. All passengers and crew must wear safety belts which should be securely fastened and checked by the crew before take-off. Strict adherence to the orders from the crew chief or pilot is required for your safety.

Remember that helicopters are loud and vibrate a lot when in flight. Flying comfortably in a helicopter takes time and exposure for you as well as your four-legged partner. Some dogs will *never* get used to this. Plan on early training and frequent exposure to minimize the concerns of the dog and yourself and be familiar with helicopter safety precautions to minimize accidents and injuries.

COMMERCIAL LODGING

It is one thing to stay out overnight in the field or at base camp with your dog; it is an entirely different matter to take the dog into a motel to spend the night. Motels and hotels have strict regulations regarding dogs in the rooms. Some facilities readily accept dogs, others require a pet deposit, while some will refuse to admit the dog to the motel.

Don't be too judgmental of those places that do not accept dogs. They've usually allowed animals in the room in the past but have had negative experiences with dogs as guests; either there were damages or else the room was left in a shambles.

I have heard horror stories from motel personnel regarding guests with dogs. One particular motel suffered almost five thousand dollars in damage incurred by thoughtless dog owners who allowed their dogs to chew furniture, teethe on paintings, soil the carpets, tear wallpaper off the walls, and destroy drapes and shower curtains.

Dogs should not be left unattended and unconfined in a motel room. Crate the dog or leave it in your vehicle if you are leaving the room to prevent careless or uninformed housekeeping staff from startling the dog or leaving the door open, allowing the dog to escape.

Carry a clean blanket, sheet or a towel with you to give the dog a place to sleep. Allowing the dog to sleep on the bed is not a good idea but if you insist on this, please remove the bedspread so that it doesn't become soiled. Make sure that the dog does not damage furniture, and feed the dog in the bathroom on the floor to minimize the mess from the water and food dishes. When we spend the night in a motel, the dogs are quite content on the floor or in their crates. This practice prevents me from being paralyzed in bed by three hounds sleeping across and alongside me. Remember, a big dog prefers ninety percent of the bed!

Cleaning up after the dogs is just as important outside as it is inside. Carry plastic bags and paper plates for picking up fecal matter, and dispose of it properly. Some motels will direct you to the closest place to walk the dog while others will have a place clearly marked for exercising dogs. The careless or negligent dog handlers in the world have made motel life for dogs almost a thing of the past. Creating a positive image occurs when you pay particular attention to details and leave the place in as good as or better condition than you found it.

I encourage dog handlers to actively work towards the recognition of SAR dogs as public service dogs. This designation allows qualified search dogs to enter any public building and to make use of public transportation but the key to acceptance is having a well-behaved, socialized dog at one end of the lead and a conscientious, socialized handler at the other.

Keep track of the motels at which you have gained acceptance and follow up with a letter if the service deserves it. A little positive feedback goes a long way.

BUILDING A SEARCH AND RESCUE TEAM

Once you have made the commitment to work in the field and either have a trained dog or are in the process of training your dog, you may want to be associated with an established SAR group or to start one on your own. Working with a group of people gives handlers the benefit of others' experiences to establish training and testing standards and forms a working team for responding to actual missions.

Established groups should have existing by-laws, an established structure, officers, and training standards as well as an accessible group of working handlers with whom to work and learn. If you want to develop a new group it will be important to determine the goals of the group and build the mission and by-laws towards those goals.

The disadvantages of joining an established group include adapting to organization styles and training standards, existing group struggles, politics and different working methods. Check into the background of an established group before jumping in with both feet. There are a lot of self-proclaimed experts out there so be discerning, but keep in mind that most SAR groups can benefit from the experience, energy and ideas of new members.

The disadvantages of developing a new group include a struggle for power, establishing common goals and training standards and agreeing on the overall direction the group will take. A new group may struggle for acceptance by agencies that call out dog teams; however, the group will quickly gain acceptance if a structured presentation of the skills and abilities of the group is made available.

It is important to formalize the organization only if the group as a whole decides that it would be in their best interests. Once this decision has been made, establish the formal structure by electing officers and setting the meeting structure, goals, objectives and standards for the group.

By-laws should be written to define the mission statement of the group, membership requirements, elected officers and responsibilities, meeting order of business, clarification of dues and costs, and other pertinent issues.

I would strongly urge that the new group clearly define training and qualification standards, call-out eligibility and discipline guidelines. Without clear eligibility guidelines, struggle between group members is always a potential. If the group is to have a newsletter or training bulletin, the costs of duplication and circulation must be considered; dues and initiation costs should reflect these expenses and should be reviewed annually.

Training and mission readiness should be the main focus of any search and rescue group and every SAR group should be actively involved in public service and education regarding wilderness survival, prevention of outdoor accidents and preventing people from getting lost. Despite this focus there are several groups that combine interests, coupling SAR with showing (conformation), obedience and public awareness and there are some groups that combine all of these interests.

Because any search can turn into a crime scene and since investigations require good detailed reports, adding record-keeping requirements to the club rules and regulations will help reduce personality conflicts.

Training guidelines and qualification standards are also important facets of a group. Determining how a dog will progress to being qualified for call-out is important to define at

Waiting at base camp.
PHOTO BY JAN TWEEDIE

the onset, recognizing that it is always possible to update standards as time and abilities progress.

I advise groups to prioritize communications equipment as the second most important item of business following the establishment of training and qualification requirements. It is mandatory for SAR groups to have current and capable portable radio equipment that will allow the teams in the field to communicate with the coordinator and each another. A simple hand-held, multi-channel portable radio is the most common means of communication. These radios cost anywhere from $250 to $1,000 each. Check with other local search groups to determine what kinds of radios and the radio capabilities they are currently using.

The cellular telephone is a new piece of communications equipment that has recently become affordable, making immediate contact with other searchers possible. Car phones range in price from $25 to well over a thousand dollars. There is a monthly service charge which varies from carrier to carrier as well as a charge per call that is usually cheaper than a pay phone. Some companies will give non-profit agencies a break on equipment and fees.

Some groups choose to jointly fund vehicles, compasses, packs and field gear and leave them in a mutually agreed accessible place for all members. Identification cards (preferably with a photo) are also recommended.

Contact other SAR groups and ask for copies of their by-laws and training standards to help you get started on yours. Equipment lists, contact names and addresses can also be obtained from existing groups. If possible, get on the newsletter mailing list for other dog groups. Other newsletters will give you training ideas and may assist in the development of a call-out system and by-laws as well as keep you informed of other groups' activities and missions.

Annual training seminars are available across the country and vary in price from under $100 to very expensive. The National Association for Search and Rescue (NASAR) holds an annual conference at various locations in the United States and they can usually recommend specific lecture and training tracks for SAR dog groups.

Contact your state and local SAR organizations and arrange to attend a meeting or meet with them to introduce your group, goals and abilities. Most SAR communities have SAR councils which are comprised of one representative from each member group. Some of these councils hold mock searches on an annual basis to provide training, certification and activities for the groups. Some groups are required to re-certify each team member on an annual or biannual basis while others are never tested. If permitted, your group may choose to send a representative to the area search and rescue meetings to get to know the other groups and to become involved in the council. Often these area SAR councils will have annual fundraising events and assist groups in getting started. The SAR council is often the foundation group for all call-out and response to missions.

The Schmitt Team.
PHOTO BY KAY SCHMITT

FINANCING YOUR SEARCH TEAM

Since most SAR groups do not receive outside funding or support, the costs for radios and equipment must be borne by the membership. As a result, fundraising becomes a key element in most SAR groups. Most teams receive minimal support through contributions from the public and handler contributions, or a grateful victim may donate money. Occasionally a group may qualify for a grant from a civic organization, but most groups utilize membership initiation and annual dues as a means of maintaining a small operating fund. Some groups have also been successful gaining support contributions from area merchants and businesses.

There are a number of successful methods for obtaining funds including, but not limited to: garage sales, bake sales, labor auctions (group members are "bought" by individuals to perform yardwork or housework for a specific monetary donation) and donation cans planted in supermarkets or malls with the permission of the management. Many creative thinkers have come up with unorthodox but highly effective ways of raising money.

There are some private agencies and foundations that will grant money for the purchase of specific equipment and if you are interested in finding corporate money, check with your local library for grant listings. The grants you are interested in should be listed as money available for community welfare, children's welfare, and outdoor services. There are thousands of dollars in grant money that go unclaimed every year.

One major drawback to receiving grant funding is that the granting foundation may require specific reports or attach strings to the funds. These strings can range from a simple annual report to monthly reports, public speeches or formal report presentations. In addition, if you do not fulfill the requirements of the grant, you can be forced to repay the foundation.

Unfortunately, the truth of the matter is that search and rescue teams cannot rely on outside donations or grants. The handler is expected to foot the bill for 99 percent of the team's expenses. Sometimes handlers can deduct expenses (such as mileage to and from training and searches, special equipment and travel expenses) as non-cash, charitable contributions on annual tax returns but you should get help from a qualified tax authority before claiming these deductions. There are loopholes but some basic things like the actual purchase price of the dog or annual vaccinations cannot be deducted.

Keep an accurate record of all expenses related to the dog team with ongoing expenses such as dog food, shelter, construction of a run or training site, and mileage on searches and training recorded in detail. Other expenses like special vehicle equipment, crates, and special working equipment for the continued operation of the dog team may be deductible so keep receipts for these items and keep these records in chronological order to be inspected by the Internal Revenue Service if requested.

Some agencies will repay the handler for search-related expenses including fuel, transportation, food and lodging, but there are usually very clear limits as to what will be repaid. If the team requires repayment for expenses be sure to state that up front so that the agency knows what to expect. Restricted budgets may prohibit an agency from repaying expenses and may ultimately be the deciding factor determining whether or not the agency can afford to call the dogs.

If an agency is going to repay you for expenses, you must keep receipts and fill out an expense voucher to get repaid. Keep a notebook in your vehicle for recording mileage and storing fuel receipts. If you get in the habit of documenting expenses, it will be easier to get repaid.

Several years ago, resources tried to assign an hourly fee to show the amount of money saved when volunteers were used on searches. In 1974 a search dog team was worth $25 per day. In 1994 a trained search dog team was worth at least $50 per hour because of the specialized training involved. A typical wilderness search can last for several days involving many volunteers and several dog teams. If you multiply $50 per hour times 24 hours (two twelve-hour search days) times the number of dog teams, it is clear that the costs would be prohibitive.

It would be rare for an agency to have the funds to pay for a two-day search and if it becomes necessary that you receive payment, you may find yourself out in the cold. If you got into the search and rescue business to make money, I highly recommend that you rethink your priorities! It is not feasible, nor rational, to expect an hourly wage for performing a voluntary task. Remember, the purpose of search and rescue is *"So Others May Live."*

GLOSSARY

The following glossary will clarify some of the terms and words used in the text of this book. The definitions presented here are user-oriented. Terms may have more than one definition or interpretation.

ABC
American Bloodhound Club. This is an organized group of Bloodhound owners and fanciers. It has over 600 members worldwide. The club sponsors show, obedience and trailing events.

AIR SCENT
The ability of the dog to pick up any available airborne scent. This also describes one of the two divisions of search dogs.

AKC
American Kennel Club. This organization registers purebred dogs and keeps records and information regarding registered dogs and recognized breeders.

ALERT
The physical signal given by the dog to the handler indicating a find, a recovery, a problem, a scent pool or the end of the dog's trail. This varies from breed to breed and dog to dog.

AS THE
CROW FLIES
The distance between two points measured in a straight line regardless of terrain features or actual ground distance.

BASTARD SEARCH	A title given to a search effort after it has been determined that the lost person was either never missing, not lost, intentionally gone, or was found completely outside of the search area. This includes searches which are launched based on false or inaccurate reports. A bastard search is also called when the person being sought actively evades or hides from the search teams.
BERM	The surface and vegetation along the side of a road. This is often grass, gravel, dirt or other natural material that holds scent.
CADAVER SCENT	Scent material from the decomposed remains of a human being which is obtained through a licensed medical examiner prior to the victim being embalmed. Cadaver scent is usually refrigerated or frozen between uses.
CADAVER SEARCH	A search for the remains of a deceased person or, in criminal searches, the search for burial sites or fragmented remains of a victim.
CAST	When a dog is air scenting or attempting to pick up a trail, the dog will sniff the air in a circle or pattern to locate the available scent. The wind will carry scent from the victim. The dog moves his head side to side, up and down, "casting" for a scent.
CATCHMENT	A place where scent will pool, usually a natural barrier such as an undercut on a bank, a hole, the downwind side of a rock, or a berm along a road.
CIRCLING	When a dog circles around attempting to locate the strongest scent available.
CLAIM	When the trail ends with a victim some dogs will stay with the victim until he or she is safely out of trouble. The dogs show claim by licking the victim or tagging the victim with their noses.

CLUE

A clue is anything which contributes information, direction of travel or leads to the finding of the missing person. The clue can be anything from a footprint to a note. Scent is the intangible clue left at every crime scene and at every point the lost person passed. Scent is overlooked in 99% of crime scenes. Clues can be gathered from interviewing, trackers, sight lines, etc.

COLD TRAIL

A trail which is aged or where scent has been adversely affected by weather or time.

CONTAMINATED

When the scent article or the trail has been crossed or handled by another person or thing that is not the subject of the search.

CUTTING SIGN

Footprints or other clues which indicate the direction of travel of the lost person. This is often done by professional mantrackers.

DEM

Department of Emergency Management. In Washington State, this office handles the call-out of search and rescue resources for law enforcement agencies.

DEM#

Department of Emergency Management mission number. This number will be preceded by the year and the next available chronological number. A DEM# is assigned to all search and rescue and training missions. Labor and Industries insurance covers volunteers while on registered searches which have a DEM# assigned.

DES

Department of Emergency Services. Same as above. (Used to be known as the Dept. of Civil Defense.)

DOT

Direction of travel.

ESAR

Explorer Search and Rescue, a division of the Boy Scouts of America. This group provides ground and evacuation teams for searches.

EVIDENCE	Part of a crime or crime scene. This may include stolen articles, fingerprints, footprints, blood, or weapons.
EVIDENCE SEARCH	The search for any items of evidence which may be used in the prosecution, charging, or disposition of a criminal.
FIND	When the search dog locates the person or evidence being sought.
GEAR	All equipment and hardware necessary for the handler and dog team. This includes radios, harnesses, leads, water, etc.
GRID	A section of land identified on a map. A grid may be defined by township, range and section or through a series of map and compass measurements. A grid may be based on latitude and longitude as well. Grids are used to establish a specific area or location.
GSSD	German Shepherd search dogs. A SAR dog organization which utilizes German Shepherd dogs as the primary search dog.
GUN SHY	A dog who expresses fear, hysteria, or paranoia at the sound of a gunshot.
HANDLER	The person who works and is responsible for the search dog in the field.
HARNESS	A configuration of leather, nylon webbing or other such material which allows the handler to restrain and control the movement of the search dog. Some search dogs are handled on-lead only and most handlers of on-lead search dogs place a harness on the dog to avoid pulling on the neck. Harnesses should fit the dog without causing injury and should be made of washable material.
ID	Identify. A dog in training must make a positive identification of the correct "lost" person.

LEAD   A long leash made of a non-stretching material (1"
                doubled nylon web) which ranges in length from
                18" (traffic lead) to a 20' field lead. The most com-
                mon SAR leads are 4', 8', 12' and 15'.

MARKED TRAIL   A trail on which the runner leaves markers at all
                turns or changes in direction. This may include
                flagging an area where articles are dropped. A
                marked trail helps the new handler learn to watch
                the dog for changes in body language (alerts) to
                show what has occurred on the trail.

MAST   Military Assistance to Safety and Traffic. The US
                Army provides a crew and helicopters to airlift
                injured persons and search teams on missions.

MEDIA   Television and newspaper journalists as well as
                other publication and voice professionals who
                broadcast or report newsworthy information to the
                public.

MISSION   A search and rescue call-out or search.

NASAR   National Association for Search and Rescue. This
                is a national organization based in Washington,
                DC. The organization is comprised of search and
                rescue volunteers and paid personnel from around
                the world.

NASAR DOG   National Association for Search and Rescue
ALERT   newsletter. It is published every six weeks and
                contains training ideas, general information and
                mission reports.

NPBA   National Police Bloodhound Association. Made up
                of law enforcement and corrections personnel, this
                group offers annual training seminars, a newslet-
                ter and assistance in locating Bloodhound han-
                dlers and breeders.

NWBSAR	Northwest Bloodhounds Search and Rescue. Northwest Bloodhounds was founded in the mid-'70s to direct search teams to assist law enforcement agencies in searching for lost persons. More recently, they have established written certification requirements for dogs and handlers. This group provides a monthly newsletter and information to members and interested persons.
OVERSHOT	When a dog goes over or beyond the actual trail.
OWNING A FIND	After a search dog makes a find, the dog will often remain with the victim and appears to expect that the person will be his to keep!
PLS	Place last seen.
READ	The ability of the handler to understand the physical clues from the search dog which indicate a fresh trail, cold trail, deceased person or imminent find. Most signals from the dog are specific to the individual dog and range from tail movements to the pace of the dog. The handler should be able to tell when the dog has reached a scent pool, located a turn or has located a break in the trail.
REWARD	The piece of liver, cheese, or attention given to the dog by the handler following a successful training exercise or search.
RUNNER	A person who lays a trail and hides from the dog on a training trail. Also called "quarry."
SAR	Search and rescue.
SAR COORDINATOR	The person, usually a law enforcement officer, who coordinates the overall search and calls the resources out on a mission.
SCENT	The intangible trail of invisible cells which are constantly being shed by the body. Scent drifts with wind, adheres to brush or remains on the ground. Adrenaline will increase the level of scent.

SCENT ARTICLE   The item used to start the dog on a trail. The scent article can be personal clothing, a vehicle seat, a footprint, a location where the subject sat down or a ledge, window sill or other such physical location where the missing person was seen.

SINGING   The baying or whining noise made by some dogs as they trail. The sound increases as the dog approaches and finds the missing person.

SUBJECT   The person the dog is seeking.

SUBPOENA   A court order issued to a witness in a criminal proceeding. Refusal to appear may result in the witness' being arrested and charged with contempt of court.

TRAIL   The path of scent which the dog follows to find the missing person.

TRAINING TRAIL   A practice search designed to exercise the SAR team's abilities. As the dog increases ability, the trail is made more difficult by adding obstacles, aging the trail, or adding crossing runners who intersect the victim's trail.

VARI-KENNEL   A metal and molded plastic crate used to transport dogs. The crate must be large enough for the dog to stand up and turn around.

WATER SAR   Search and rescue mission for a person missing in the water, as in a drowning.

Anxiously awaiting the next trip!
PHOTO BY BETTY HENSLEE

OTHER SOURCES OF INFORMATION

For more information here are some additional resources for you to use as you train and expand your skills and abilities.

Books

The New Complete Bloodhound
by Cathy Brey and Lena Reed.
This book covers general history of the breed, health care, feeding, breeding and has some information on showing and mantrailing with a Bloodhound. There are several short profiles of handlers and their dogs.

Practical Scent Dog Training
by Lou Button.

Go Find! Training Your Dog To Track
by L. Wilson Davis.
Written to help the AKC tracking enthusiast; however, general information regarding scent and scent theory is helpful.

Tracking Dog: Theory and Methods
by Glen R. Johnson.
General overview of systems and methods for starting a tracking dog.

SAR Dog Training
by Sandy Bryson.
Designed for the air scenting search dog. This book contains good general information about working with search and rescue dogs.

Dog Owner's Home Veterinary Handbook
by Delbert Carlson and James Giffin.
An "owner's manual" of sorts for dealing with medical aspects of dog ownership.

How To Raise A Puppy You Can Live With
by Clarice Rutherford and David H. Neil.
This is an excellent puppy training book. It will help the new owner start general training on the right foot and encourages positive training methods.

Manhunters! Hounds of The Big T
by William Tolhurst as told to Lena Reed.
A selection of stories and missions worked by Bill Tolhurst and his Bloodhounds.

Meet Mr. Grizzly
by Montague Stevens.
Using Bloodhounds to hunt bear, Stevens discovers the trailing abilities of the Bloodhound. This is an old book that is out of print.

ORGANIZATIONS

American Bloodhound Club, Inc.
Corresponding Secretary Ed Kilby
1914 Berry Lane
Daytona Beach, FL 32124
This is a national breed club encompassing Bloodhound enthusiasts who breed, show, work and enjoy Bloodhounds.

American Kennel Club, Inc.
5580 Centerview Drive
Raleigh, NC 27606-3390
This is a purebred dog registry with contacts for most breeds.

National Association for Search and Rescue, Inc. (NASAR)
4500 Southgate Place, Suite 100
Chantilly, VA 20151-1714
Internet address: http://www.nasar.org
The national *SAR Dog Directory* can be found here, which lists SAR dog organizations by state and specialty. Contact specific groups for membership, training or newsletter information.

PERIODICALS

AKC Gazette
This is the official journal for the sport of purebred dogs published by the American Kennel Club. Subscription information can be obtained from the American Kennel Club, 5580 Centerview Drive, Raleigh, NC 27606-3390.

American Bloodhound Club *Bulletin*
Published by the American Bloodhound Club on a quarterly basis. For information, rates, or to obtain copies, contact Brenda Howard, ABC *Bulletin* Managing Editor, 616 Texas Street, Suite 101, Ft Worth, TX 76102.

NASAR Dog Alert
This newsletter, published by the National Association for Search and Rescue, features articles and information on search and rescue dogs, teams, and missions. For subscription information, contact NASAR, 4500 Southgate Place, Suite 100, Chantilly, VA 20151-1714.

Dog World Magazine
This is published by PJS Publications, Inc. For subscription information, contact P.O. Box 56240, Boulder, CO 80323-6240.

EQUIPMENT AND SUPPLIES

Big Red Search Supplies
2009 Green Parks Drive, Ellensburg, WA 98926-2074
Features harnesses, leads, collars, and limited handler supplies.

Search Equipment Company
P.O. Box 70626, Richmond, VA 23255-0626
Phone 1-800-473-4901.

Brigade Quartermasters
1025 Cobb International Blvd., Kennesaw, GA 30152-4300
This company sells outdoor clothing and equipment suitable for search and rescue work.

R.C. Steele, Inc.
P.O. Box 910, Brockport, NY 14420-0910
Features dog equipment and supplies.

PET USA
P.O. Box 325, Topsfield, MA 01983-0425
Features dog equipment and supplies.

JB Wholesale Pet Supplies, Inc. (New Jersey
1-800-526-6388

New England Serum Company, Inc.
P.O. Box 128, Topsfield, MA 01983-0228

K-9 Specialties
1-800-363-5236

INDEX

ABOUT THE AUTHOR

A native of the Pacific Northwest, Jan has done what everyone dreams of: she has combined her vocation of law enforcement and corrections with her avocations of dogs and the outdoors. Jan currently works as the Chief of Corrections for the Kittitas County Sheriff's Department in Washington State. She works and trains her Bloodhounds for search and rescue and criminal work, often going out on calls in the middle of the night to find a lost hunter or to uncover evidence or a criminal. Beginning with her first Bloodhound "Digger," she has continued to learn through veteran handlers, seminars and experience and she continually shares that knowledge with many other enthusiasts. She often is called on to work with new handlers, law enforcement, attorneys and civilian agencies as well as to speak to groups. This book is a result of the letters, phone calls and training sessions requesting more and more. She resides in Ellensburg, Washington with Ben and Kailey and spends a lot of time on the road training and trailing. Jan is the National Trailing Trials Chairperson for the American Bloodhound Club and is spearheading the effort to gain acceptance of Bloodhound Trailing Trials as a recognized sporting event. In addition she holds memberships in several search and rescue organizations, breed clubs and canine groups.

1/02

On the trail!

GAYLORD M2